Enterprise-Wide Software Solutions

Enterprise-Wide Software Solutions

Integration Strategies and Practices

Sergio Lozinsky

ADDISON-WESLEY

An Imprint of Addison Wesley Longman, Inc.

Reading, Massachusetts • Harlow, England • Menlo Park, California
Berkeley, California • Don Mills, Ontario • Sydney
Bonn • Amsterdam • Tokyo • Mexico City

Many of the designations used by manufacturers and sellers to distinguish their products are claimed as trademarks. Where those designations appear in this book, and Addison Wesley Longman, Inc. was aware of a trademark claim, the designations have been printed in initial capital letters or all capital letters.

The author and publisher have taken care in preparation of this book, but make no expressed or implied warranty of any kind and assume no responsibility for errors or omissions. No liability is assumed for incidental or consequential damages in connection with or arising out of the use of the information or programs contained herein.

The publisher offers discounts of this book when ordered in quantity for special sales. For more information, please contact:

Computer and Engineering Publishing Group
Addison Wesley Longman, Inc.
One Jacob Way
Reading, Massachusetts 01867

Library of Congress Cataloging-in-Publication Data
Lozinsky, Sergio, 1955–
    [Software, tecnologia do negócio. English]
    Enterprise-wide software solutions: integration strategies and
practices/Sergio Lozinsky.
        p.   cm.
    Includes index.
    ISBN 0-201-30971-8
    1. Application software. 2. Business—Data processing.
I. Title.
QA76.76.A65L69   1998
005.3′068′7—dc21   97–44128
                                                                 CIP

Text printed on recycled and acid-free paper.

ISBN 0-201-30971-8
1 2 3 4 5 6 7 8 9—MA—0201009998
First printing, March 1998

For Sônia, Adriana, and Fernando

Contents

Foreword

Business and technology: currently these two components of the corporate world are practically one. Every company is trying to be more competitive and to reduce its operating costs as a passport to becoming a player doing business in tomorrow's markets.

This situation, related to the absolute need to build feasible critical mass in almost every business segment—thus imposing the need for larger volumes of production and services—and the need to fulfill ever increasing and sophisticated client requirements have created the opportunity for companies to develop technological solutions that could support making radical changes in other companies' business processes so that they can address the new and challenging market reality.

Business application software—or business application packages—are the stars of this new scenario. Not so long ago, almost every corporation was developing its own management information systems by itself, trying to implement systems solutions that were perfectly designed and suited for its unique business requirements. Well, things have changed fast. Now selecting and implementing the most appropriate software package to support the company's business processes is considered a *best practice,* since the new packages can supply the data and the controls a company needs to manage its activities. Companies have discovered that they can't be good at everything. They must achieve outstanding performance in their *core* businesses in order to survive and be successful; but for the activities that support those *core* processes, it is better to evaluate whether the market can offer something more powerful and reliable than the internal knowledge, experience, and structure can produce—and perhaps at less cost.

Uniqueness does exist, and in fact it is responsible for failures and successes in the market. But for many other internal processes, the problem is to determine the benchmark to be pursued, which means doing things the best possible way, not just doing them right. The answer probably lies in some solution already achieved by a competitor or another company in a different business segment. *Best practices* have become a goal for most companies. To get there, a company needs systems that are designed based on *best practices concepts,* which are methods that have proven efficient and effective for carrying out necessary activities with the least cost and the best results.

Best practices are one reason why the application packages industry has grown so much. Being aware of this phenomenon, software vendors have spent billions of dollars in research and development to bring to the market products that can help companies get to this new level of competitiveness, where ongoing improvement is a must.

As technology becomes easier to use, thus meaning that there will need to be more complex technical architectures running underneath what the user sees (in order to provide the simplicity of operation), management information systems development will require more specialists, larger investments, better productivity tools, and proven methodology. This constitutes a new *core business* all by itself.

Technology has become easier to use, almost intuitive, once implemented; the complexity has migrated from the end user interaction with the systems to the development and implementation side of these same systems.

Selecting the most appropriate package, and having a successful approach to implement it, is one of the most important challenges facing companies that are pursuing this new level of operations. And exactly as we have said before, the situation of radical change brought on by the implementation of these packages requires extra careful attention from company executives and adequate preparation by the project team and users involved. The rewards—as represented by the benefits obtained from a successful implementation project—are immense. Operating costs will be reduced, thus guaranteeing excellent return on investment; more productivity will be possible with larger volumes of work; improvements in access to information will make for more agile decision making and better negotiating with suppliers and clients; there will be no need for reworking reports or reconciling accounts; reliable figures will be available to analyze business performance; morale will improve; a bright future lies ahead.

But this future is not to be had for free. Besides the natural costs of the products and the services, there lies a key ingredient: the organization, approach, and commitment to the implementation. It's not just a matter of gathering good brand names and paying money to make them work. As Sergio Lozinsky writes in this book, there needs to be a *tripod*—the software vendor, the hired consultants, and the company. Each one needs to play its specific and noninterchangeable role in the course of the project.

Enterprise-Wide Software Solutions: Integration Strategies and Practices was originally written in Brazil, a country that has experienced a major change during the last few years. Coming from a hyperinflation situation and a protected internal market, the Brazilian government realized that the country needed to attract foreign investments to reverse the economic situation and provide better opportunities for the people (SAP itself opened its Brazilian subsidiary in 1995). To make the country attractive for investors, there needed to be stability, a potential market for goods and services, and fair competitive rules. The Brazilians have had success in their efforts, and they continue to make the necessary adjustments.

For Brazilian companies, both local companies and multinational subsidiaries, these developments meant speeding up all the plans to stay competitive in their markets. There was no more room for doing things *gradually.* The software package market experienced an incredible demand as a result, and today Brazil is one of the most promising regions for growth in the next few years, as is Latin America in general.

Having worked with software package implementations for a long time, Sergio Lozinsky is totally involved in this current boom of software packages in the region. Perceiving how executives and company professionals in Brazil were not aware of what is really involved in a software implementation project (and this is also true for the global market), Sergio decided to write a book explaining what he has learned from his practical experiences. This reference book is designed to prepare companies to make a decision about investing and monitoring a fundamental change in the company, through the use of a new business software application.

It is interesting to pay attention to the subtitle of the book "Integration Strategies and Practices." Sergio is not presenting a new implementation methodology or stressing the need for specific support tools to help develop the work, or even comparing products from the market. He is concentrated on discussing the points that must be addressed by the company acquiring a software package to make the implementation project successful, and to assure that the expected benefits will be in place at the right time. This means gaining an understanding of what should be done when first evaluating the idea of acquiring a business software application; how to make sure the project will get *everybody's* commitment, and not be the challenge for a small group of heroes; what can be done to pick the most appropriate package; how to differentiate among the consultants called to participate in the bidding process; who, from the company, should be assigned to work on the project in order to assure that there will be sufficient knowledge to pass on to future users; how to deal with customization demands; what helps in getting the commitment of end users during the training and testing phases; how to monitor the software vendor *after* buying the package; and more important, after the project is finished, how to partner with other companies using the same product.

So that the company's expectations can be satisfied, and to make sure that the wonders presented during demo time will be in place when the system goes into operation, the proper equipment should be installed and adjusted; basic data will need to be reviewed and defined; business processes may need to be restructured; professionals will have to be trained; new personnel may need to be hired; and everything must be tested all together in order to check that the system works satisfactorily.

This book covers the essence of results-driven package implementation and distinguishes that from more mechanical package installation approaches. Results are defined in terms of schedules, cost, minimum disruption, and business benefit. The roles of process reengineering, transition management, and other nontechnical activities, and their integration into the systems development life cycle, are described in straightforward language, and clearly related to project success.

The text is very readable. It takes the dry, technical discussions of implementation methodologies and represents them in layperson's language, with a relaxed tone and an easygoing, informal narrative. You don't have to read every word. To keep the reader's attention, Sergio uses plain, down-to-earth language and peppers his narrative with examples, colorful language, and interesting and relevant quotes from famous people.

For a typical large software implementation project, I would give a copy of this book to all project participants—including members of the Executive Committee and any other key decision makers—at the beginning of the project, if not before. I would request that they read the book from cover to cover, then reread key sections on the stages of implementation as the project progresses.

This book does a good job of giving the reader an idea of the kind of issues that a company will face along the way, so that there will be a chance to anticipate and perhaps avoid some of the more common issues and there will be fewer surprises to look forward to.

Paul Wahl
CEO of SAP America

Preface

This book addresses the evaluation, selection, installation, implementation, use, and economic advantages of using business software packages. In the United States and all over the world, companies are installing software packages for business automation at an unprecedented rate: financial, manufacturing, distribution, and, *primarily,* integrated packages, which promise to cover all internal functions in one product. Most of the firms and their corporate officers who purchase these packages are not experienced buyers of such products and related services. This book establishes a baseline for planning and managing expectations between corporate managers, their information technology staff, and outside consultants.

The human issues are critical here—not the technical ones—and the human issues are less likely to change quickly. Although automation has become a tool kit for every manager at every type and size of organization, there is little material available to guide the journeyman in how to implement, use, or manage these tools. The distributed, integrated, automated environment has become an avalanche that threatens to sweep up the business community; it has already outpaced the educational mechanisms necessary to support it.

The book is a guide to what to expect when a company is getting ready to purchase and implement a new software package. It provides an "A to Z" perspective of the many technical and nontechnical elements that must be considered. It provides a framework for implementing all the bits and pieces that make up a system.

Experience shows that the real problems with business packages are comparability (evaluation and selection), evangelism (getting corporate consensus), training and motivating the end users, and maintenance (support, extensions). These issues are very well covered by the author.

This book can be read and used to establish a "common language" among groups of people who rarely speak the same language today: senior business managers, information technology managers, information technology key users and end users, and external business consultants.

Companies are spending significant amounts of money and time to implement business package solutions. This book can be of tremendous value to the business community by helping readers reduce the necessary costs and time required to install new company-wide software to more reasonable levels.

Acknowledgments

I am deeply grateful to all those who helped me bring this book from idea to print. Special thanks to Marco Parillo, who developed some key contacts in the United States, which led to discussions with Addison Wesley Longman. Marco also reviewed the original English version; his careful reading was essential to ensure accuracy and consistency. I would also like to thank Timothy Birnley, William Girling, Peter Patton, and James R. Wagner for their review comments.

Many thanks to my editor Mary O'Brien at Addison Wesley Longman, who helped bring a technical book written in Brazil into the U.S. market. To Eduardo Salomão, my editor in Brazil, who was the first one to believe in the project, and published the book in Portuguese.

Finally, I'd like to thank my wife Sônia for her support and encouragement throughout my work on this project.

1

Making the Decision to Acquire a Software Package

The Idea of Acquiring a Software Package

With each thought we have, we create our future.
—Louise Hay

Today, in the second half of the 1990s, to think about substituting a company's existing information systems with software packages is not such a revolutionary idea. Reengineering, quality control, the outsourcing of services, the technological evolution that has simplified the interaction between the layperson and information technology applications, or *informatics*[1]—all are common business practices. So, too, is the development of client-server environments, because human resources are valued as the principal factor for sustaining business success, and because these environments make possible the democratization of access to information. All of us are equally familiar with downsizing, the pressures of rising costs and decreasing profit margins, as well as many other phenomena generated in the world of business. All of these phenomena give software vendors opportunities for developing and marketing sophisticated, "ready to use" information systems. A combination of research and administrative talent,

---

1. Brazilian Portuguese has coined the term *informatics* to signify "the application of information technology." We will use it throughout this text.

1

as well as technology and marketing, make possible the design and development of such systems—and they are generating business investments that have already reached into the billions of dollars.

Today it is reasonable to believe that it is just a matter of time before a company will make a decision to acquire a new software package that promises efficiency and cost savings. The need will arise simply because in the current information technology environment certain unnecessary costs are no longer sustainable. The results obtained using outmoded systems—the quality of information available to the company—do not present a return compatible with the investments made. In summary, companies are losing competitiveness by employing expensive systems that are approaching obsolescence.

Many factors are leading companies to seriously consider the possibility of replacing their information systems with software packages. Most reach this conclusion after confirming that they must reduce costs to remain competitive. Another factor that influences companies to implement new software packages is the observation that everybody—the competition and other businesses with which the company maintains relationships—is already on this same path. In the section entitled "How Will the Company Benefit from the Acquisition," we will see some of the more common objectives companies pursue when they decide to buy a new software package.

The previously mentioned point—the quality of the information derived versus the costs of maintaining the present systems—is the basic question executives need to address when they evaluate an investment in a new software package. They can classify the idea of information quality into various fundamental aspects, some of which are listed below in the form of questions:

- Are the company's present systems really working tools that have been incorporated into the way the company does business and intrinsically linked to operational and management activities, or do they serve more to record what has happened for later (at times, *much* later) analysis?

- Is the data that is presently reliable available, as generated by current systems, or does the company depend on doing reconciliations, revisions, or even manual adjustments at the close of the month to make the numbers acceptable?

- Is the company's evaluation of its financial position based directly on results obtained from the present systems, or is the evaluation based on worksheets derived from reports generated by these systems (normally produced by expending a great deal of additional effort)?

- Are the various business processes of the company naturally integrated (finance and accounting, purchasing and accounts payable, sales planning and production, receiving, fiscal books, inventory and costs, and so forth) in the present systems? Or, do these functions operate solo and, consequently by default certain people are assigned the responsibility of ensuring that the information flow is consistent?

- Is the number of persons involved in support activities reasonable as compared to those at other companies with similar business volumes?

- Are the response times for client requests satisfactory? Is the necessary information available?

- Does the company's experience with suppliers, recorded by the present systems, add value when it comes time to negotiate new contracts?

- Are the present systems really used in the company's planning process?

Obviously, this list does not exhaust all possible concerns associated with the quality of information, but it does provide an initial framework to suggest how present systems should be evaluated. Let's now add to those questions the following:

- How much does it cost the company to maintain such systems at their present level of contribution to the business?

- Is this cost-benefit relationship satisfactory?

- How much would it cost to migrate from the present situation to an environment of "ideal" systems, based on software packages?

- How much would it cost to maintain such an "ideal" environment?

The key to making a decision on investing in software lies in comparing the present quality of information plus the cost of achieving this quality to the investments needed to improve the quality of information through software packages plus the cost of setting up the new environment.

When a company has spent a large sum on informatics but has not achieved a great deal through its information systems, deciding in favor of change is easy. The problem comes with investment capacity. When the quality of information is low, but the costs associated with the current system seem reasonable, or the market risks of standing put are not particularly threatening, it is necessary to analyze just how long the company can survive using this mode of operation before a significant investment in its business processes and systems will become imperative. On the other hand, the present quality of information may be satisfactory, but the maintenance cost is believed to be excessively high.

Generally, today's companies are not satisfied with their current systems. On the average, their systems were developed over a decade ago. In spite of being chronologically recent, these systems are now part of the distant past, once we take into account the requirements imposed upon businesses by today's global market. Moreover, the role of technology (systems) in businesses has also changed. The role of technology has evolved from simply supporting operations to become an integral part of the essence of the business. As a result software vendors have had the opportunity to develop sophisticated, all-encompassing, and integrated, software *packages*. Businesses value these packages as short-term solutions (when compared to the alternative of developing such integrated systems with in-house personnel) in their struggle to maintain and expand markets and profitability.

If, despite these facts, people in your company believe it would be better to start developing systems using internal resources—people who understand the company and its peculiarities—remember, in order to create systems that permit the company to compete in the current market, the in-house professionals will have to thoroughly understand the concepts of MRP II, ERP, supply chain, preventative maintenance, distribution control, activity-based costing, financial management, business simulations, traceability, auditing trails, career and succession planning, and executive information—just to cite a few of the concepts that must be considered in the design of system functions. Evidently these concepts are evolving. Company leaders must take into account such evolution to adequately maintain systems and keep everything current and useful. Otherwise the companies can soon regress to their previous situation.

Clearly, many companies have personnel in their information technology group who can absorb the necessary knowledge and who have experience in developing sophisticated systems. The problem is that such specialized computer work is usually not the main business of these companies. They should be directing all their available resources into improving their own products or services so that they can better serve their clients and continue to have the necessary competitive edge.

Since designing and implementing integrated software packages is not the business of most companies, or a focus of their executives, the systems their internal personnel come up with will never equal the quality, scope, or technology of those created by software firms whose business this is. Computer software firms can produce sophisticated packages and provide clients with products that allow them to maintain a focus on their own chief activities, thus improving revenues, profits, and stockholder returns. Yes, companies should think about developing their own tailored systems, but only insofar as adding functionality to the best packages they can find. Any customizing would concentrate on those functions that are really unique to the company's particular business processes, functions that guarantee the company advantages over its competition. Such functions can be thought of as "technology for better market positioning."

This combination of investment in good packages and technology that gives the company the leading edge is the model that provides the greatest return on the significant and continual investments associated with businesses meeting the increasing demand for informatics.

Overcoming Resistance and Shifting Paradigms

Men would do greater things if they didn't believe so many things impossible.

—Malesherbes

The initiative to acquire a software package is usually not shared from the start by everyone in the company. Until a few years ago, such a lack of consensus was not a big problem, because the process of finding packages occurred in isolation, by department. Individual departments did not have to concern themselves with what the rest of the company was doing.

With the arrival of *integrated* systems, and the absolute need to consider what they can do for everyone in the company (which I will detail in the next chapter), the promotion of such systems before leaders and opinion makers from all sectors of the company has become indispensable. After all, during the software implementation process the participation of everyone involved is basic to the success of the implementation project.

But it is during the presentations that the first obstacles arise, as evidenced by these typical reactions:

- "Our business has peculiarities that no package can deal with. We're different!"

- "I don't know about you, but my department is being very well served by current systems. Maybe it's just a question of improving on what we've already got."

- "I've already worked in a company that tried to implement a package. It was a real disaster!"

- "We'll become forever dependent on the company that sells us the package. They're always going to figure out ways to add new costs for us so they can maintain product support!"

- "In this information technology market, software companies rise and fall all the time. What happens if we're left holding the bag?"

- "Technology is moving so fast. We hardly understand the equipment we've got, and now it's becoming obsolete. Wouldn't it be better to wait just a little longer?"

- "I worked in a company that started using a package. We once had to wait an entire week to send out invoices because the product had a problem!"

To combat these reactions, it is necessary for members of the company to be shown the other side of the coin, so that obstacles can be transformed into challenges. The commitment of top management to the idea is fundamental.

Directors must present the vision they have in mind for the company. They must be able to persuade employees that modernizing internal processes is important in order for the company to continue to grow and profit in the market. The advantages to be enjoyed by everyone based on the successful implementation of the new software package must be made evident to all. At the same time the problems related to the current systems and processes need to be pointed out. Among these might be duplication of work, difficulties in obtaining information, the need for reconciliations, overtime work to close out the month, and an undesirable dependency on analysts and programmers who hold absolute power over certain critical systems. Since these functions do not add value, the company should eliminate them when implementing a sound and integrated new information system.

Visits to other companies that have already employed solutions similar to those candidate systems company leaders have in mind may help to create a more realistic view of the project ahead. The main message to communicate is that the implementation process is complex, requires dedication, and problems do occur, but the results are worth it, because the right system can help create a more efficient work environment.

Yes, it is true that certain current functions may disappear when the new system is put in place. Nevertheless, as compensation the decision to implement a package also creates enormous opportunities for the company's professionals who will become experts in applying the new technology to doing the firm's business.

The issue of opportunities and drawbacks is a controversial one. It is easy to see that automating business processes through technology can eliminate the jobs of many staff members whose function is to record, control, calculate, compare, file, or prepare reports. More difficult to see is that this same trend creates windows of opportunity for professionals because they can unfetter themselves from the way that things are still done in most companies. They can start to prepare and position themselves to become highly valued individuals in a new working environment that will demand completely new functions, functions in which the use of the technology at hand, relationships with clients and suppliers, the generation of added value to the company's products, the constant updating of know-how, and a multidisciplinary approach will become the differentiating factors in evaluating leaders.

This same trend is creating opportunities not only for the companies that adopt new technologies but also for hundreds of new businesses that were unimaginable just a few years ago, businesses that are springing up all over the place, betting on the demand for innovative products and services developed from ideas that continually strive to expand the possibilities for applying these new technologies. Professionals, companies, and all levels of government must become more aware of this process in order to, respectively, become more pro-active in the field of personnel training, restructuring business, and restructuring education in general, by seeking to take maximum advantage of what these new opportunities offer society.

In every software package implementation project in which I have participated, I have found people who believe in this vision of the future. Once they dedicated themselves to the project they earned promotions, improved their salaries, and increased their visibility in the company (and, often, outside the company as well).

Is It Going to Be Very Expensive?

Almost everybody knows how to earn money; only one in a million knows how to spend it.
—Henry David Thoreau

The question about costs is difficult to answer. The size of the investment needed to move from the current situation to a future situation with a package running in an appropriate environment can vary substantially, depending on the type of system chosen, the technology involved, whether the company takes advantage of existing equipment to a greater or to a lesser extent, whether the company outsources the current MIS department services during project implementation, the level of internal resources available for doing the work, and many other factors.

One may conclude generally that the investment will be significant, starting at several hundred thousand dollars for medium-sized businesses, and going up to several million dollars for large corporations. Once the advanced functionalities and advantages offered by a software package are understood, it is the cost-benefit relationship that the company should really be analyzing. A well-selected, integrated system that has been correctly implemented usually pays for itself in a relatively short period of time—between six and thirty months.

The quick return on investment is estimated based on the fact that the company can expect an average administrative cost reduction of 30 percent with the advent of the new system. Hundreds of companies engaging in software package implementations around the world have chosen this level of cost reduction as the average. My experience shows this is true for large corporations, but usually smaller enterprises have less fat to burn. Anyway, the savings are impressive and should be evaluated in order to make a realistic forecast of the project's potential benefits.

It is worthwhile to conduct a modest feasibility study to quantify some of the potential benefits the package could offer. This study is a means of briefing top management, obtaining commitments, and creating a favorable climate for going forward with developing the project. Many companies conduct a feasibility study using internal resources, at times, informally. In other cases, they call upon specialized consultants to present a formal analysis to the board or shareholders, in order to win approval for the investment.

A factor in favor of all who contemplate investing in new software packages and new technologies is that the prices for software and equipment have been declining over the past years and are continuing to fall, mainly owing to intense competition. On the other hand, the cost of consulting services associated with implementation (the topic of Chapter 3) remains stable, and for certain more complex packages it has become significantly more expensive because there is a shortage of qualified people and because preparing such people to participate in these projects requires a significant investment.

How Will the Company Benefit from the Acquisition?

Sow benefits, reap praise.
—Ricardo Palma

Returning to the question of perceived improvements and advantages, the decision to invest in new systems and technology must be based on perceptible and tangible benefits for the company. Here, again, many possibilities exist, depending on the historical evolution of the company, its present structure, the quality of its human resources, its current systems, and many other factors.

Generally speaking, we can cite some objectives companies seek in implementing new software packages:

- to drastically reduce the size and cost of the company's informatics sector;

- to decentralize information processing by making data available in real time where the company needs it, without the user depending upon "overnight runs" or requests to the MIS department;

- to provide technology tools that permit substantial simplifications of the processes involved in the accounting, finance, fiscal, and general administration functions, as well as the generation of management reports in order to diminish the costs of providing the structure needed to maintain the processes of control and business management;

- to create a base so that the company's billings can grow while the costs of providing the corresponding internal support become proportionally less than they are at the current level of business;

- to achieve a better balance between decentralization and control, so that when the company provides the various sectors (sales, purchasing, technical assistance) greater resources to exercise their functions, the company can avoid duplication, ensure synergy, and manage the indicators that permit evaluating actual market performance;

- to meet the demands made by major clients to decrease product and service costs and become electronically linked with them in order to exchange information and orders;

- to be a pioneer in the employment of new technologies, or to apply technology similar to that which the company's principal competitors are using.

The importance of having quality information systems available is of such a magnitude that a brief brainstorming session among executives and technicians will reveal these and innumerable other business objectives that should be considered when searching for new tools and technologies.

Obtaining Everyone's Commitment

I'm interested in the future because that's where I'll be spending the rest of my life.
—C. F. Kettering

The decision to acquire a software package requires the support of the leaders and *key users* in all sectors of the company. These principal users of the systems must be involved in the implementation process. Their clear commitment to the decision to implement a new software package is vital. With everyone's participation, the project will *belong* to everyone, and not just to a small group of people who are out to prove their hypothesis, while the rest of the company sits back to watch the initiative as if they were attending a Roman circus and waiting for the lions to attack and devour the Christians.

It is not necessary that everyone be euphoric about the project, but they should work pro-actively and collaborate so that everything comes together. Although it is hardly possible to eliminate personal and political considerations in most companies, they cannot be allowed to take precedence over the imperatives of the business. After all, everyone will benefit from the fruits of the implementation project.

A good way to obtain strong commitments is to establish a package evaluation team (a Decision Makers Committee, about which I will speak more in Chapter 2). It should consist of representatives from various company sectors; together they will be charged with reporting to top management on the alternatives selected. By using such a team the employees will get the idea that the project belongs to everyone and that the final decision will be based on concrete and measurable factors, not on subjective factors. Having a team also addresses early on the even larger issue of integrating sectors, because the new system will require such integration in order for the system to work correctly.

As stated previously, the attitude of top management with respect to the acquisition process is fundamental. The evaluation team must readily perceive in top management, as well as all who will be part of the process, that there is a strong commitment and vision for the company, and a willingness to remain involved, among other things.

In some companies or business groups, in order to lend additional importance to the process of selecting and implementing a software package, the company generates a document that formalizes everyone's commitment to the project. Figure 1.1 illustrates such a pledge of commitment to a package implementation project. Representatives of the various company units or functions, as well as the contracted consultants, obligate themselves to the initiative's success by signing the pledge.

Planning the Selection Process

Having made the decision, ensured the commitment of all (or almost all), and generally understanding the challenges to be faced and the time frames involved, it is time for the company to go out and find the ideal package.

As a first measure, it is necessary to decide whether the company wants to work alone, counting on the talent and dedication of its personnel, or if it will contract with consultants to help the evaluation team in the selection process. There are certain advantages to using consultants in the selection process. For one, their input is a way of bringing proven methodology to the decision-making process and guaranteeing a degree of technical impartiality. Moreover, a consulting team can dedicate its time totally to the selection process, thus partially freeing up members of the evaluation team to carry out their normal work.

Also because the contracted consultants should have had experience in selecting and implementing packages, they can contribute practical information about software vendors and their products. This experience can help to focus the efforts of the company on what is really important, and add objective factors to the decision-making process.

Obviously, contracting with consultants at this stage of the project means additional expense, but the investment might be money well spent, in the

[Name of company] has made the decision to use state-of-the-art technology, and is dedicated to reviewing its business processes to obtain better management and to control information at lower costs.

To this end, a process of selection and acquisition of a software package that meets the majority of our company's needs has been initiated and should be implemented by [date].

Being aware that the successful implementation of such a package requires the:

- commitment of top management;

- participation and dedication of the system's future users;

- backing and support of information technology personnel;

- acceptance of the product's natural limitations;

- development of interfaces with current operational systems and with those under development;

- effort of consultants, with due respect for the know-how and culture of the company; and

- spirit of collaboration on the part of all;

we, the undersigned, reaffirm our commitment to the success of this project.

We shall seek to implement processes efficiently, make resources available, make decisions necessary to lend continuity to the work, and collaborate among ourselves to transform this challenge into a benefit for [company] and to the professional satisfaction of all involved.

Figure 1.1 Project Xxxxx—Commitment to Success

sense that using consultants may increase the degree to which employees participate in the process: Everyone will take note that a formal project is truly underway, one that involves outside support.

Some companies start with a simpler selection process. For example, their decision makers might look at what most of their competitors are using. They might talk with colleagues in other companies who are knowledgeable about good packages that are available in the market, although these colleagues may be in very different lines of business. Then the decision makers might call in one or two vendors and request demonstrations, so that the evaluation team can form an opinion about the products.

Nevertheless, I recommend that with or without the help of consultants the company adequately prepare itself for the selection process. Most vendors of software packages can make presentations that leave potential users dazzled, and without proper consideration the selection may end up being based on a set of factors that are insufficient for arriving at a well-grounded decision. Knowing how to listen and look is essential. Above all, it is vital *to know how to ask questions*. During a vendor presentation, asking a question for which an overhead transparency does not exist might lead to nuances being revealed that permit adding a few points to (or subtracting a few points from) one's initial enthusiastic evaluation of a particular product.

Asking good questions means not taking anything for granted: Are all the functions that are being presented totally available (or will they be part of the next version)? If available, are any other companies already using them? What types of arrangements can the vendor make to integrate third-party products that complement the software package? How is training organized? How long before the training courses should be booked? Could the vendor show how a certain type of operation works in the package?

2

Selecting the Most Appropriate Package

There Is No Perfect Package

Common sense: the quality of those who think like we do.
—Roberto Dualibi

The idea that there is no perfect package needs to be very clear for everyone in the company. The selection process does not have as its objective finding the software package that meets every requirement imagined by the users, 100 percent. That means that the software should be flexible while meeting the company's needs; the software package is not meant to be "tailored to fit."

Every software package that exists in the market grew out of the experience (or opportunity) of a group of people working in a specific business who created systems that could deal with certain business segments adequately. As practical questions of implementation arose, the scope of activities of their products grew. The concepts were expanded upon, and new functionalities were introduced into the software through research and collaboration with third parties. Software vendors copied good ideas from the competition, and they relied on consultants, user suggestions, and so forth. Yet each package has a history that, in sum, determines in which type of businesses it can best be put to work.

In the latter part of the 1990s we are witnessing an era in which many software packages have evolved to the point of presenting themselves as solutions to a wide spectrum of business challenges. This phenomenon is more obvious for administrative-financial functions, but we may still note important differences among packages designed for dealing with manufacturing functions, for example.

It is the notion of integration that permits the company to obtain significant benefits for its administrative processes, by eliminating redundancies and controls that are no longer necessary in an integrated environment. The most important requirement is that a software package generates an *integrated system*. As part of their design, integrated systems allow information to enter at a single point in the process (for example, at the materials receiving stage of a manufacturing process) and update a database for all functions that directly or indirectly depend on this information (for example, in materials receiving, we have inventory, fiscal books, accounts payable, costs, general ledger, and treasury). The integration should take place in real time, not through interfaces or programs that transfer information to one or more modules only after the information has already been processed and updated in the module through which it entered the system. Once placed into the system, the information should be available in all the necessary forms through which it may be accessed, throughout the system.

When we think about the company as a whole, it is possible that some packages, upon analysis, will not cover the desired scope. In this event, it is important that the vendor of the product already have concerned itself with establishing partnerships with vendors of complementary products and that the technical problem of integrating the different products be already resolved, or that they be in the process of being satisfactorily resolved, so that solutions will be available within the time frame desired by the company.

In conclusion, the company needs to develop criteria that permit the evaluation of candidate solutions. To choose the best system, the company needs to measure, with precision, the degree to which the candidate packages meet the business needs of the company.

Has the Technological Environment Already Been Predefined?

The technological environment is a matter that can simplify and also complicate the software selection process. For some companies, the choice of a package determines the data processing environment the company will adopt when it implements the solution (the equipment and technology required to run the software). Other companies will already have a predetermined informatics strategy (this is common among subsidiaries of multinational corporations). This circumstance will limit the company's latitude in selecting among the universe of packages, since the software must be compatible with specific equipment and technology the company has in place (a package determined by the selected technology).

Today the distance between these two extremes is decreasing rapidly, since new technologies are of an open nature, and there is greater flexibility for integrating software into different data processing platforms. Thus, during the evaluation phase, decision makers have more products to choose from, even though their company may already have defined the operating system, the database, and the brand of equipment to be used. Meeting the business requirements should take precedence over selecting the preferred technical infrastructure. A general rule is to try to work with products that do not depend on certain platform technologies. That way the company can preserve its investment in the event that it becomes necessary to alter or substitute data processing environment components.

With regard to the processing environment, there is good news and bad news. The good news is that the number of alternatives for the company to create its technological infrastructure (servers, operating system, telecommunications, databases, E-mail, workstations, and so forth) has been expanded significantly. Because of competition, the quality of the products has improved, and prices have dropped. The bad news is that many components are required to build the necessary infrastructure. Some are hidden within others, requiring a complex process of planning, evaluation, negotiation, guarantees, management, and monitoring. This complex process needs to be supported by specialized technicians who can independently vouch for the solutions that are selected. One strategy that can be of help is absorbing the practical experience package vendors have gained in developing their products and installing them for other clients: What environment is more useful? What is recommended? Have formal partnerships been established between the software vendor and other technology vendors whose products will be needed to build the infrastructure?

The hardware/equipment supplier with the best solution for developing the infrastructure to process the software package may not have been the best only a few months before. Furthermore, nothing guarantees that this firm will continue in the future. For example, in the area of computers, firms that just a few years ago were on the brink of failure have introduced new products that revolutionized the market, reversed their situation, and forced competition to try to eliminate the differences imposed by these innovations.

In the field of technology, absolute guarantees do not exist. It is necessary to always keep planning horizons within view (because nothing lasts forever) and to bet on partners who have proven that they are prepared to continue evolving and competing in this market. That means that company decision makers must always return to the previously posed question of the cost-benefit relationship: What can the company expect as a reasonable return on the investment—and how long will it take?

How Can the Selection Process Be Simplified?

The market offers many options, and new products are always cropping up to make the task of selecting a new package even more difficult. Selecting among an enormous variety and number of packages is inefficient, considering that the company will need to reach a decision within a relatively short period. (In most companies, the window is about two to three months.) Thus, dedicating more time to evaluating fewer products is a better idea; that way the analysis can be more in depth.

To weed out some of the choices, members of the Decision Makers Committee need to establish preliminary criteria so as to arrive at a maximum of four products for detailed analysis. (I have worked in some projects in which the decision was to do a detailed evaluation of only two packages, and in my experience cases have also arisen in which the selection process was transformed into a confirmation process for just one single, preselected candidate.)

The preliminary selection criterion must, naturally, be few. Nevertheless, they must be specific and provide sufficient information to discriminate between options and determine whether or not the candidate packages provide the solution to the company's needs. In order for products to qualify, the company's requirements should be met or not met—not met to some extent or approximately or the like.

What must be considered among these preliminary requirements? The answer varies a little from company to company. Typically, the requirements must reflect those aspects that future users consider indispensable for the successful conducting of business or to the company's culture. Here are a few examples:

- The package must have an ample base installed throughout the country (at least twenty installations), so that the company does not become part of a club of laboratory rats who will have to go through the process of ironing out the problems typically faced by the vendor because the product was only recently introduced into the market.

- The cost of the package must be less than x number of dollars, because of the company's investment limit.

- The package vendor must provide local support (physical or through a remote link) with a guarantee of an acceptable level of timely service for the company.

- The package must be international, having proven to be successful in various countries, although it may have been introduced into the company's region only recently.

- The package must provide, clearly and verifiably, certain functions considered to be mandatory for users (for example, the ability to deal with multiple currencies; the capacity for doing simulations; the ability to make an allowance for electronic communications with clients, suppliers, and banks; and so forth).

- The package must provide customization tools so that the system can be adapted to meet the needs of the company, without "damaging" the software's architecture.

- The package vendor must be well positioned in reports published by technology market analysts, such as the Gartner Group, and Forrester and Patricia Seabold. These reports normally list how much investment the software developer continues to make in the product; in the technology market such ongoing investment is a question of life or death. Some companies put more than 20 percent of their revenues (yes, revenues) into systems improvements so that they can continue to be competitive in a market in which their products can become obsolete within a few months.

We can include the above examples in the more detailed list of requirements to be drawn up when the decision makers evaluate the preselected candidates (as we shall see below). During the preselection phase, the idea is to establish requirements that are absolutely nonnegotiable, so that the company can discover right from the start of the process which vendors and products have no chance of competing. In this manner, company decision makers avoid wasting the company's time and money.

How Can Products Be Compared without Mixing Apples and Oranges?

There's no such thing as a commodity. All products and services are differentiated.
—Theodore Levitt

Once the software packages that have the best chance of meeting the company's needs are chosen in the preselection phase, it is time to start a detailed evaluation process. This process will permit the making of a purchasing recommendation to the board or stockholders who, ultimately, must free up the resources so that the company can move forward with the project.

One way of organizing the selection process, keeping in mind the previously mentioned idea that *the project belongs to everybody,* is, as we have said, to create a Decision Makers Committee. Key people from the various sectors of the company who are recognized and respected as leaders and opinion makers should make up this committee. The role of the committee is to make the final recommendation on the package, to be directed to the company's top management.

Intuitively we know that there needs to be some common basis for comparing packages, one that permits the effective measurement of the advantages and disadvantages of each package with respect to the others, thereby establishing a technical basis for making a decision. Various routes are possible for arriving at this common basis of comparison, which will be an extensive and detailed list of functional and technical requirements. For example, members of the Decision Makers Committee might conduct interviews with personnel from various sectors to reveal certain needs and characteristics important to the company's business. Workshops are another, perhaps preferable, way to derive the same information. The Decision Makers Committee might convene a meeting of various people from the management and operational levels, associated by function, area of activity, or business process to discuss for a few hours how their piece of the business works, what problems they face, where they encounter weaknesses in the current system that a good package could help to make easier, more efficient, or more effective.

The idea of holding a workshop is interesting for various reasons: first it can help reinforce the notion that the project *belongs* to everyone, and it furthers the idea that a commitment from everyone is needed to make it happen; and, second, it can be a forum for discovering ways to replace current systems with the new system, thus freeing the company from old assumptions and procedures that have persisted for years because no one ever questioned them. A wide-ranging and uninhibited discussion about how things work may turn up many activities that fail to add value to the company's business. These processes should be eliminated or at least given low priority. Interestingly, many of the activities that fail to add value are exactly those functions that some people see as setting off the company as *completely different* from all others. Through this process, some may end up discovering that the company is not so different as people thought.

Well-conducted workshops generate a list of mandatory and desirable requirements that everyone shares and, simultaneously, these sessions serve an educational and cultural function. They send out messages about the future systems environment users can expect to experience.

This list of product requirements will include items such as

- flexibility to set prices according to different criteria;
- the ability to deal with financial information in dual currencies;
- minimal information needed to grant credit;
- defining software system aspects that are inherent to the planning of the company's business;
- the ability to treat consignment and sample items; and
- the capacity to control commissions of sales representatives.

A list of requirements can reach several hundred items covering operational and management functions that the package, ideally, must provide.

It is even worth considering organizing a workshop for top administrators so that they can refine definitions of the company's characteristics from the perspective of the overall management of the enterprise. They can explain the goals they intend to achieve by implementing the chosen package.

At the end of the various workshops that the company will sponsor, those conducting the selection process will be handed a lengthy list of requirements, organized by functions: accounting, finance, production planning, service, sales, and so forth.

At this point the Decision Makers Committee comes back into the picture. Each member of the committee will have participated in one or more selection workshops, and, from now on, each member will represent a group of users during the selection of the best package.

As the first step, committee members will attribute relative weights to identified requirements, according to each member's idea of how important these requirements are to the business. In this manner, each product will be assigned a score that reflects how it meets the company's most critical requirements (remembering that no package is perfect).

Then the committee can set up dates for package vendor presentations, so that decision makers can compare products. Committee members should avoid pressuring vendors to present their solution in just a few hours; for integrated systems, a presentation can last days. Given adequate time for presentation, each function of the package can be evaluated in detail. For such presentations to be effective and so that they can be compared more efficiently, it is useful to send all vendors a list of the company's requirements beforehand. Then the vendors can tailor their presentations to demonstrate how their product can appropriately address each of the listed items.

An additional list of requirements (not to be provided to vendors) should be prepared by the Decision Makers Committee, or by those directing the project. It should include questions regarding how well each vendor performs the product presentation, how much knowledge about the product its presenters displayed, the quality of the materials distributed, and other aspects the company considers relevant for evaluating a potential business partner.

All future company users should attend presentations of only those modules associated with their specific functions. But committee members should be present at all presentations, so that they can form a complete opinion on each product and understand the pros and cons of each solution, from the standpoint of the business as a whole.

During these sessions, or shortly thereafter, all of those present should assign each product a score based on the degree to which the product meets each requirement, according to their individual understanding. At the end of the session, once the software vendor has departed, the project leaders need to conduct a discussion to arrive at a single, joint score, which will become the official and formal result of the software analysis for the selection process.

Arriving at a Consensus

No explanation is sufficient.

—Karl Popper

Once the selection process has monopolized everyone's agenda during several weeks (and probably after many complaints have been made to the effect that everybody is making sacrifices so that the project can go forward), the company decision makers have by this point derived an exceptional base of opinions and technical data for continuing on with the decision-making process.

Some companies at this juncture will schedule visits to other companies that are using the selected software package, as suggested by the vendors, and the decision makers will subsequently add a few more requirements to their list based on what they observe during these visits (such as the quality of the support, problems the other company experienced during package implementation, user satisfaction, benefits achieved, and so forth).

Contact with other companies that are already using the product can be very useful, especially if it is possible to identify similar business needs and processes for the purposes of comparison. But when making such visits, it is necessary for representatives of the Decision Makers Committee to keep in mind that people are not quick to admit their mistakes because of pride. So in order for the information gathered from these visits to be effective and reliable, it is necessary for company representatives to ask the right questions to ferret out where the potential problems lie in using the software.

Generally questions should be designed to gather information about the following items:

- the type of support provided by the vendor;
- the qualifications of the vendor's support personnel;
- the extent to which alterations can be made to the package to tailor it to the needs of users;
- the reliability of the product;
- the vendor's response time when called to resolve problems;
- product performance;
- where the product's functionality is the strongest;
- the product's functional and technical limitations;
- the time required to implement the package; and
- how the package has evolved (improvements made to the product) since the other company acquired it.

Then the Decision Makers Committee must meet to decide. Readers may be wondering, Decide what? Didn't one of the packages get the highest score? Then why not simply deem it the winner, since the evaluators have already gone through such a complete and exhaustive process? Well, it is true that one of the packages must have gotten the highest grade, but this by itself is not enough to call it the winner. Very probably, if the preselection process was conducted thoroughly, even the packages with lower grades would have met the needs of the company reasonably well. They just were not quite as good as the one with the highest score when it came to certain requirements that are given great weight by the company (sometimes in but one or two of these requirements). Probably, the software with the highest score also left something to be desired in a couple of areas. (Remember, the perfect package does not exist.)

Having gained a thorough understanding of the differences between the products, the Decision Makers Committee will then evaluate which solution is best for the company (the one that will bring the greatest benefit), through open discussion among its members. They will try to visualize the advantages and disadvantages of each candidate solution that has achieved a minimum reasonable score. It is here that such issues as costs, implementation time, the technology involved, and identification with the vendor and product, as well as other factors, come into play and lead to one product being favored over others—not necessarily the product suggested by the numbers alone. Those factors may not have been given a weight in the evaluation process because they depend on benefits that can be forecasted in association with each solution. Even if they cannot be precisely calculated, these benefits can be estimated through the degree to which they can help fulfill certain key business requirements or critical success factors.

At this juncture, above all, it is fundamental that there be a consensus. For those whose opinion ends up being rejected by the majority, it must be patently clear that the choice was made by the group as a whole, and that the company will need to count on everyone's goodwill to achieve success as the process moves on to the software implementation project.

3

Getting Help with the Implementation of the Software Package

Can the Company Develop the Implementation Alone?

It's necessary for us to help each other. It's the law of nature.

—Jean de La Fontaine

Let's put the question another way: What does the company need to carry out the implementation of the software by itself? To successfully set up the systems—that is, to carry out the work correctly and within a reasonable time frame—in-house people assigned to the project must have certain knowledge and skills. To start with, the company needs to have on hand several people who are thoroughly familiar with the product and with technical issues, because implementing software means evaluating the best value to assign a specific parameter, or optimizing a forty-digit structure to define a chart of accounts, for instance. The software selection process cannot possibly supply company personnel with this kind of know-how. Experience has proven that to become an expert in a sophisticated product, a good professional will require six months to a year of training, and part of this training must necessarily consist of having the opportunity to participate in a software implementation project.

Some of you may be thinking, Well, in that event, we could ask the product vendor to place someone at our disposal, part-time, during the implementation project to train and provide support for our personnel. Some vendors provide this service as a way of showing that the cost of implementing their product is less than that of the competing vendors, whose packages require greater support and take longer to set up. Some vendors (but not all) may suggest a risky approach with a lower service cost just to sell the package. For integrated and sophisticated software, this approach is a mistake, and it carries a high price. Although the price of using this approach may seem imperceptible at the start, it will become clear as schedule deadlines are missed because the project team is not able to conduct the scheduled activities on time. Sometimes the deadlines will be rolled back because *hidden* tasks arise that no one had thought about previously (or for which the software vendor failed to provide any warning).

Some software vendors have their own consulting teams, whose responsibility it is to develop the implementation work following a standard approach. Without a doubt, these teams know the product and can be of assistance in its implementation. But producing good software and developing services for implementing the software are two different propositions. Both require significant investments. A software vendor that tries to be the best at everything ends up hurting its own business and spreading its investments too thin, and such a vendor may compromise the future competitiveness of its own product along the way. Moreover, as we shall see in Chapter 4, specific roles exist to be filled by each partner involved in the package implementation project (the company, the software vendor, the consultants, the specialists), and these functions are carried out better when there is no conflict of interest (the implementation team frequently faces questions about which the software vendor and the company hold divergent opinions).

Besides having a thorough knowledge of the product, the people who implement the new software package need to have other vital qualifications (know-how and abilities). Among these are, for example,

- knowing how to organize an implementation project from the beginning to the end. The project team should be able to present a proven methodology that allows everyone to foresee how they must carry everything out in proper sequence, to guarantee that the company achieve its objectives for the project and that the return on the applied investments occurs on schedule.

- having available experienced personnel who know how to deal with the problems that naturally will arise throughout the project, and how to handle a predicament such as knowing when to adapt the software to the company versus adapting the company to the software.

- using professionals who understand the techniques of project and workshop leadership to ensure the participation and commitment of appropriate personnel in an environment that is perceived as impartial.

- having people with management experience in projects of this nature to guarantee that the work plan develops properly and that the work is done within the budget for the desired investment.

Given the increasing pressure to reduce the number of people on the payroll and to focus increasingly on the company's core business, it becomes ever more difficult for a company to assume total responsibility for implementing an integrated software package. Furthermore, the idea that the company must invest in preparing its personnel to conduct software package implementation on its own runs up against the argument that the return on such an investment is dubious. Worse still, in the short run there is no apparent possibility for leveraging this know-how in other lucrative opportunities.

As we shall see later, the idea is to concentrate the company's efforts, instead, on preparing its personnel to administer the package *once it is implemented*. Once these employees have been trained, they may participate in replicating the implementation of the software package in other units of the company, in order to reduce the additional investment in training, should this prove necessary.

In summary, the participation of company personnel is fundamental and critical, but the company must plan that participation so that its people play an appropriate role in the project. The company should bring in the know-how and experience that will guarantee the best possible use of the acquired package, as well as provide sound support for users.

How Can a Consulting Firm Help?

What's really necessary in a company that provides service is to have people who like people.

—Frank Petro

Business consultants are professionals who specialize in developing techniques and methodologies for dealing with the processes, administration, management, and the informatics of companies that are their clients. Each consulting firm—especially the larger ones, the so-called Big Six (Andersen Consulting, Coopers and Lybrand, Deloitte and Touche, Ernst and Young, KPMG Peat Marwick, and Price Waterhouse)—seek to serve the largest possible spectrum of business segments, covering such diverse areas as finance, production, human resources, and marketing by presenting themselves as qualified to develop the solution their client desires. All of them have consulting practices that leverage their accounting expertise in the areas of business systems information technology. But in practice a point made in the previous section remains valid here: The professionals who are to be assigned to the project need to have proven experience in the type of service the company seeks. Consultants must have been trained in the methodology of software implementation, have already worked on similar projects, and, specifically for software packages, thoroughly understand the product.

Certain consulting firms, having forecasted the high demand for integrated packages that was to come several years ago, invested a great deal of money in developing a range of consulting services in this field, and assigned many professionals from their ranks to become not only specialists in the implementation of software, generally speaking, but specialists in the implementation of certain specific products. These are the types of consultants who are most important in the context of the present discussion. These firms researched products available in the market, talked to vendors, developed an understanding of their plans, made suggestions for improvements in the identified software, confirmed that the vendors' packages worked, and spent large sums to gear up to serve the market that would be generated by the sales success of the software packages in question.

Thus when we talk about contracting with consultants to help in the implementation of the selected package, we are talking about contracting with people who have made this business their focal point for generating revenue and profit. We refer to companies that plan to amortize their investments in personnel training over many projects; thus these are companies that can offer the market a combination of product and implementation at a cost that would be less than what the client could expect to spend in developing a similar solution through using its own internal resources.

Therefore, to the extent that a company decides to select and contract with consultants who really have experience in the implementation of the package it has selected, these professionals can add value to the project, and the company can obtain the additional know-how that will be most useful in its future initiatives in the field of informatics or in process reengineering. More information on evaluating potential consultants will be provided in chapters 4 and 6, where we look at the consultant's role and the organization of the project.

Will Hiring Consultants Be Expensive?

So many things are more important in life than money. But boy are they expensive!
—Groucho Marx

So here we go again with a question about costs. Well, it is reasonable that we continually raise it, because, after all, we are not talking about a small amount of money, and, moreover, every project that involves technology presents a certain amount of risk. So we have to ask this question—always.

Let's recall our statement from Chapter 1: In reality, once we understand the improvements and advantages of a software package, it is the cost-benefit relationship that we should analyze. A well-selected, integrated system that we have implemented successfully usually pays for itself in a relatively short period, between six and thirty months.

If you still have not yet realized it, you will be surprised to discover that the cost of hiring consultants to implement the package is precisely the most expensive part of the proposition. For integrated software of the latest generation, the cost of consultants starts at $1.50 and can reach $3.00 for every dollar invested in the software product. Incredible as it may seem, when I spoke about a quick return on investment, I was already taking into account the total project cost, that is, including the cost of hiring consultants to help with the implementation.

Independent of all the reasons presented previously for using a consulting firm, this reason alone—the cost of the service—is sufficient to point to the importance of seeking out the right consulting partner to assist in the implementation process. Consulting firms normally charge for the time their professionals spend working on a project. Thus, to try to reduce this cost, it is important that the contracting company know how to absorb part of these hours by having its own people take care of tasks that do not necessarily need to be performed by consultants, leaving to those providing the consulting services only those tasks that really demand specialized knowledge and that add value to the project. Among the tasks that can be absorbed by the company's professionals is the programming of interfaces with other systems, the preparation of data conversion programs, and the training of operational users. I will return to this topic in the next chapter, where I address the role of each player in the project's development.

Contracting for the Software and the Training and Implementation Services

Each Party Has a Role to Play in the Project

When there's partnership, domination doesn't exist. The parties involved in the same situation share their abilities and talents to achieve a common goal. They walk together toward this goal, conscious of the process that this implies. This is the true partnership, one in which differences are revealed to be absolutely complementary.

—Sônia Café

The company's decision makers have done a detailed, consistent, and technically correct job of selecting a software package. They have ensured that all the business's key personnel, in one way or another, are involved and committed to the project's implementation. They have identified a consulting firm that seems to possess all the attributes necessary to conduct the implementation project satisfactorily: qualified personnel, a proven methodology, and excellent references. Is anything lacking for the project to work, for it to be a success?

Since all the ingredients are present and have been carefully chosen, the results should be quite adequate. But as with any recipe, we must carefully measure the quantity of each ingredient so that the mixture will create something that is more than a mere sum of the parts.

33

A software package implementation project does not depend solely on the software vendor, well-prepared consultants, or the dedication of the company's personnel. Success, for a project of this nature, largely depends on each party playing its role well, because these roles are singular in nature; there can be no substitution without there being a decline in the quality of the final product.

The Role of the Package Vendor

First the vendor must deliver the software and its documentation as soon as possible—the sooner, the better. Only then can the company develop the training and testing environment for the implementation team and for those users who will be involved in the project. This appears to be a simple proposition. Nevertheless, given today's open systems and client-server environments, which permit flexibility and independence in equipment, databases, and user interfaces, one frequently learns that the acquired product has not been completely fine-tuned for the data processing environment the company has selected.

This is not necessarily a problem, but the company will need to determine whether the vendor is capable of making the necessary adjustments promptly. Although the software may be installed and capable of working on the company's equipment, to get the best possible performance when it is put to use, a series of minor matters will need to be resolved. Their result will be a new, "official" version of the software. For instance, there may be questions about back-end routines; such routines are processed in the central server to achieve greater handling speed of information derived from a particular database. For the end user, no modifications are apparent, yet the software only works thanks to these apparently minuscule changes.

At times the vendor makes the necessary adjustments once the implementation work is underway. The vendor's contribution must be monitored so that the program's release occurs according to the demands imposed by the project timetable. Thus the contracted consultants are obligated to oversee this adjustment process and to defend the contracting company's interests. Consequently, they should never attempt to conceal the true stage of the work's development from the client company's management.

Another important package vendor role is to provide initial training for the company's key users, those people who will play fundamental roles as the project progresses. They are the ones who will define, together with the in-house professionals and consultants on the project team, how the software is to serve the company. In other words, they will decide how the functionalities are to be applied, as well as what the product's characteristics will be for the company's unique implementation.

Vendor-supplied training must achieve the goal of showing the key users how the package works, the principal data involved, what is flexible and what is not, how the information flows through the system, where the limitations lie, and how the software is to be used in day-to-day operations.

Some of you might be thinking, But aren't the contracted consultants also experts in the package? Why don't they conduct the training? That's true. Many consultants are capable of providing sound training for those packages they know well. That they do not lead such trainings is, again, a matter of maintaining their appropriate role in the project. The object of the initial, vendor-supplied training is to show key users how the system works, not how it is to be implemented. This means that the vendor demonstrates the product as it exists, not as the system will work specifically for the company. This latter issue has yet to be defined, because the company's personnel are not yet at a stage where they can make that determination. At this point, they lack sufficient knowledge of the problem to carry on a discussion on an equal footing with the other participants in the project (the package vendor and the consultants).

The company's key users who participate in the vendor-supplied training should try to achieve two main objectives during this stage of the work: (1) to understand the characteristics of the software; and (2) to better understand the impact the system will have on their business processes. The key users will have lots of opportunities to question the vendor during training. Nonetheless, they will eventually have to come to the conclusion that there are still some remaining concerns, and that many discussions will be needed to devise a means of guaranteeing that things will continue to work in a way that they—at the present moment—regard as "the right way to do things."

The contracted consultants also have a role to play during this initial training phase. They should participate in sessions, among other reasons, to evaluate how users react to the reality that is starting to take shape from the detailed presentation of the software's characteristics. Consultants also need to ask questions and bring up topics that perhaps the package vendor is trying to avoid. That way users will receive the most thorough possible representation of the reality of the challenges they will face during implementation. Furthermore, consultants will have the opportunity to raise issues that they, in spite of their experience, have not yet anticipated as potential impediments to carrying out the project. The insights they gain at this point can help adapt the implementation methodology to further suit the needs of the company.

The role of the package vendor does not end with the completion of the initial training; this is just the start. The vendor also plays an important project support function and must exercise quality control with respect to how the product is implemented. After all, the vendor is the one who understands the nuances of the software that could make a great difference in the software's final performance; the vendor is intimate with the subtleties that diminish (or increase) the difficulty of using the system in day-to-day operations. It is the vendor who should have the greatest interest in ensuring that every single installation of its product becomes an excellent source of referrals for potential new clients.

The package vendor will continue to participate throughout the implementation process, being responsible for validating certain definitions (those most critical) and addressing specific technical questions about the client company's technological environment. The vendor should also exercise influence in shaping this environment, principally with respect to the size and scope of the hardware to be deployed, and with the software releases (versions of databases and operating systems) that will remain in operation. These technical matters must, naturally, be discussed as soon as possible during the process, so that if the necessary hardware and software components are not on hand, they can be ordered promptly from the appropriate manufacturers and/or distributors. As we shall see later, developing the work at an appropriate pace becomes tenuous if the proper technological infrastructure is not available to the project team.

To conduct quality control properly, the package vendor should designate a specific professional from its ranks to administer this function, as well as to serve as a sort of project account manager. Even when this person cannot provide a complete answer, he or she is in the best position to find answers to questions, by seeking the support among the internal resources of his or her employer, the vendor. (Project organization is covered in more detail in Chapter 5.)

Back to our friend the vendor. The vendor has other responsibilities. As you will see in Chapter 8, project studies may determine that there are certain incompatibilities between the company's current business processes and the way the package deals with these processes, and the software may need to be customized to address these discrepancies. *Customizing* simply means altering the product so that it better serves the company's needs. The choice of whether or not to customize, as we will see later, is a delicate question, one that can have enormous impact on the project, and it often constitutes a point of discord between consultants and key users.

Nevertheless, for the time being, let's assume that consensus has been reached: customization is vital. The package vendor must then develop the necessary modifications, because only the vendor knows the product well enough to stir without spoiling it. Moreover, the vendor must guarantee that, despite any customization, the company will be able to benefit from future software improvements introduced by the vendor. Remember, part of the contracting company's return on its investment will stem from its ability to incorporate improvements to the software that expand the scope of the functionality at an incremental but small cost.

According to current practices, package vendors try to avoid customizing the product on a "client basis." They will usually try to negotiate with the customer to wait for a new release, in which the new function will be a standard attribute. But there still may be gaps in terms of what some industry segments need from the software and what it can provide. In this case, the vendor will usually agree to customize the system for those segments.

If, despite all this, the company goes ahead and decides to "open up" the package without the vendor's participation, the company could be faced with the disagreeable surprise of discovering that a new version of the product, just introduced into the market, does not fit the company's business processes, and possibly complex and costly additional interventions will be required to make it work. Worst of all, the vendor might maintain that it is exempt from responsibility in such a situation and cannot give priority to the company's predicament because, at the moment, it is fully occupied with testing and distributing the new release.

Thus, from all practical standpoints, the package vendor must be involved in any decision to customize the software. If the company opts to use its own internal resources for the customization in order to hold down the cost of this additional effort, it needs to make sure that the vendor remains committed to the result and will continue to discharge its responsibility of keeping the software operational in the future. Ideally the vendor should participate actively during any alteration of the product, and the company must respect the vendor's opinion if the company is to maintain a satisfactory relationship in the years to come.

As mentioned in Chapter 2, some packages come with a customization environment that allows the user to make certain modifications without damaging the product's architecture. But this type of customization is generally limited, because the focus is usually on permitting different views of the database, instead of allowing for the creation of new functions. Thus the package may lack sufficient flexibility to serve the company's purposes. It is this situation we are addressing here—namely, the one that demands alterations in the product's architecture.

In summary, the company cannot let itself be dumped by the package vendor as soon as the contracted software has been placed into operation. On the contrary, the contracting process must clearly stipulate that the vendor will fulfill its project role, as established, to ensure that the vendor will participate to the fullest extent possible. We will address the topic of contracts shortly, but first let's look in more detail at the roles of the other participants.

The Role of the Consultants

The role of the consultants is something that can be understood more intuitively. After all, the company places its trust in the consultants that its business objectives will be reached. The consultants are the ones who will walk away with the lion's share of the stockholders' investment in this enterprise, in the form of consulting fees. Accordingly, consultants are responsible for generating the project, that is, for administering each of its tasks so that the required activities occur at the scheduled time and at the desired level of quality, and with the effective participation of all those who must take part.

For their promises to be kept, the consultants have to transform the approach presented during the selling phase of their services—that is, their methodology—into a detailed work plan. (For some packages, the detailed plan ends up consisting of several hundred small, but important, tasks.) The project plan clearly describes what is to be done, how, when, and by whom. Sometimes the "by whom" may refer only to members of the consulting team. In other instances, it could mean company personnel working together with the consultants or even assuming total responsibility for certain tasks.

Ideally a work plan, which can be represented in a timetable or a PERT[1] chart, should be visible to all involved. (Sometimes the chart is literally hung on the wall of the project room.) That way, the roles and commitment of each player are always easily understood and visible for everyone to see. Remember, in this timetable, or PERT chart, all participants are listed, including the package vendor.

Consultants should add value to the work. They bring know-how about the package, know-how not included in the standard training supplied by the vendor. They derive their expertise from practical experience, and because of this experience the company personnel involved in the project

---

1. A graphic visualization of the tasks to be conducted, indicating their interrelationship (order of precedence), start and completion dates, and estimated hours or days of work.

can avoid pursuing ideas discarded as futile by other companies in similar implementation efforts.

Consultants should also know how to remain neutral while questioning current company processes in an effort to promote better project results. To the extent that the scope of the contracted project allows, they should strive to improve the company's business processes so that the software package can be used as it was originally intended by its developers. Refining the company's processes can only optimize the performance of the system and maximize future user satisfaction.

But improving the company's existing processes can be a delicate question, because reengineering current processes, as you shall see in Chapter 6, is a significant initiative in itself, involving a substantial investment in terms of the time and, consequently, the cost involved. Often full-blown reengineering is omitted from the package implementation project in order to avoid delaying completion of other objectives, for example, freeing up the mainframe just as soon as possible. Such considerations can lead some executives to decide, consciously or otherwise, to implement the package in the shortest possible time frame they can impose. (Generally, they want to start using the new software in the next fiscal year, yet their decision to go ahead with the implementation project is often made just shortly before the end of the present fiscal year.)

The consultants are also responsible for analyzing and clearly addressing customization issues. They must be able to differentiate between customization that is imperative, and thus must be introduced into the package during the project before conversion to the new system, and customization that is merely desirable, perhaps to be considered in the future. Worse yet, there is the type of customization that should not be undertaken, that which has only been sought out because the users still have not totally appreciated the scope of the software and remain prisoners of outdated paradigms that block perception of the capabilities of the new package. For example, consider the reconciliation of accounts that a director has always demanded in the past. This practice used to seem fundamental to the survival of the company. It no longer makes any sense to continue this practice in the new processing environment afforded by the integrated system. In Chapter 9, where we return to customization, we will look at several strategies for dealing with this issue.

Consultants also need to position themselves in such a way as to balance their loyalty to the client and project, with that of defending the package vendor, when such a defense is technically correct. Remember, the consulting firm has invested a lot of money to do in-depth studies of the software product. In a sense it has become a sort of partner of the package supplier, accredited to implement the vendor's product. Nevertheless, consultants must go beyond talking only about those areas where the product is noteworthy because of its functional and technical concepts; they must also advise the client where the vendor has problems (in technical support, for example).

To know how to walk this tight rope without falling is to practice state-of-the-art consulting. Only practical experience and market savvy permit a consultant to achieve this level of expertise. In Chapter 6 we will see that the project won't be a bed of roses, and that it is precisely for that reason that the consultant needs to know how to maneuver along this stormy course, to maintain the effort on its original track, and to see that all arrive safe and sane at their destinations. For this and other reasons, some consultants say that the greatest frustration in being a consultant lies in the fact that one cannot fire the client in order to solve the project's problems more easily.

Consultants need to steady the course by taking on for themselves tasks that should have been shared but, if not executed, would compromise the project irreparably. They need to know how to deal with internal political problems, although occasionally such problems are not clear until the project reaches an advanced stage. Such internal political disputes constitute one of the gravest threats to work of this nature. One example: Certain employees from a particular sector of the company secretly would like to see the project fail because were it to succeed, accolades would go to another sector, or to people who they consider to be enemies. (This sounds like something from a soap opera, but it does happen—and how!) Those who engage in such struggles by all appearances seem to be working in favor of the project, but actually they are working against it by subtly placing small obstacles along the way that, unless seen in time, will lead the work down a dead-end street.

Thus it is the consultant's responsibility to understand the total context of the envisioned work and to know when to alert the contracting company's management about actions and decisions that must be undertaken so that the job will not be compromised. When appropriate, consultants must negotiate changes in the project as soon as possible, when such changes become necessary owing to factors that could not have been foreseen at the time that the services were contracted. For this reason, good consultants document their work as they go along, keeping minutes from meetings, interview notes, telephone and consultation logs, samples of forms, and internal documents. They also talk frequently with all those involved, giving each equal attention and trying to maintain neutrality, to the extent that their observations should always be understood as being made on behalf of the project, and never capable of being construed as criticisms of certain sectors of the company or certain individuals.

Maintaining technical documentation on the project, which lies behind the development of all the implementation work, also falls within the responsibilities of the consulting team. After all, one day the consulting team will leave, but knowledge of the project cannot depart with it. In addressing project follow-up, Chapter 6, we will return to this point. What is important here is to remember that throughout the project the company should seek to verify that formal documentation of the work is being produced on an ongoing basis.

In summary, consultants certainly will be among those involved in the project who will suffer sleepless nights and be in a state of constant anxiety to learn about whether things are going well. This is part of the profession, and justly so. After all, if things do not go well, it is the consultants who bear the principal blame, regardless of what has happened. Nevertheless, as we shall see, what one should look for during the process of contracting with a consulting firm is assurance that the scope of services is understood perfectly by both parties—the client and the consultants—and that the rules for changing course during a project be established up front and mutually agreed upon.

The Role of the Company

The biggest obstacle to progress is not ignorance but rather the illusion of knowledge.
—Daniel Boorstin

You have probably already figured out that a project to implement a software package is like a tripod which, to stand, must be supported firmly by all three legs—the vendor, the consultants, and the company—through adequate fulfilment by each of its respective role. Therefore the contracting company has much to concern itself with and must fully understand the contribution it must make to the project, in order for the project to progress as expected. When everything is over and done, and once everyone has cleaned up the leftovers from the party to celebrate the commissioning of the new system, it will be up to the company's personnel to keep the software and the overall system and processes in good working order, according to what has been planned throughout the months and months of hard work.

The company—represented in the person of certain professionals carefully selected by top management—must act like the true owner of the project, the party most interested in the success of the work, the entity that will do anything and everything to comply with what was originally set forth in the timetable.

It may seem pretty obvious when seen in the context of this book, but practical experience has demonstrated that the company can lose sight of its role as time passes, since package implementation projects can go on for many months. Sometimes, certain people who are key to the process understand their position as being only one of demanding results and reporting problems, instead of actively participating and contributing so that the project goes as well as possible.

Soliciting the support of the contracted consultants to make the role of the company representatives very clear may work, and consultants are happy to participate in this clarification process because, as previously stated, they know that if something does not go well, it is they who receive most of the blame.

Thus it is presumed that starting from day one of the job it is necessary for key players with the company to organize and concern themselves with how to reach the desired goal. This means that the company will need to count on certain key individuals being willing to dedicate themselves to learning how to operate the software correctly to provide for the business's needs. These key individuals must acquire a certain level of technical knowledge about the product so that they constitute permanent user support for resolving simple routine problems agilely, without processing delay. Those employees who are more familiar with the system normally can recall why a parameter was registered in a certain manner, or why a procedure, previously followed by the company, was altered.

Evidently all of the company's efforts will be expedited if the consultants concern themselves with producing project documentation that will permit the employees following the development of the work to easily locate and determine the whys and wherefores. The package's manuals should also be of great help in these matters, but it is important that employees know how to use them.

In summary, one of the responsibilities of the contracting company is to learn and to assimilate information about the software package, in order to achieve reasonable independence. (That means that company personnel should need to request additional support only for problems of a higher order, problems that justify the cost of the consulting fees that will be charged to resolve them.)

Therefore, we may conclude that success in the implementation project depends partially on which company employees are allocated to the project, and to what extent they can devote their time to the project. This issue will be revisited in the following chapter.

In addition to understanding the package, the company should—and must—assume additional responsibilities. For example, it must guarantee that all users slated to participate in the project in any way, or to participate in specific tasks or phases, be made available for a part of their time at the necessary times established by the project schedule. This may involve reallocating these people's general responsibilities, although temporarily. It also means perhaps putting on hold, for the time being, everything else that is not of absolute priority. Finally, these people must be motivated by being shown that a temporary increase in their responsibilities is necessary to create a productive environment, one that will be beneficial to all concerned.

One way to maintain high motivation is to organize meetings to monitor project progress (more details on this in Chapter 7). Top executives should be present at such meetings so that key project personnel may report directly on the progress of their activities, discuss difficulties that may have arisen in the process, and receive positive feedback and, thus, encouragement to continue dedicating themselves toward achieving the expected results.

Returning to the comment I made in the last chapter about the project implementation tasks the company should assume in order to minimize consulting costs, they need to address such issues as data conversion and developing interfaces. Every package, just as in all information systems generally, is designed in such a manner that its processing presupposes the prior registry of a series of data, parameters, and tables that allow the system to function and, moreover, to reflect the environment and the specific structure of the facility in which the package has been installed.

The prior recording of information—or the initial data conversion—consists of things such as a chart of accounts, a list of suppliers, a table of payment conditions, tax codes, a registry of cost centers, a list of clients, a products list, and a great deal of other information, termed basic. Inputting the initial data requires a certain effort during the implementation of the software. Thereafter such data typically requires only light, simple maintenance. This is because the frequency and volume of updates to these files and tables is not usually significant in the course of day-to-day business operations.

Most of the information needed for this initial loading already exists in the company. Where? In the current systems slated for replacement by the package. To avoid the enormous manual task of reentering this information in the new system, *conversion programs* are developed. Basically, they read the records of the old systems and convert the information into a format that the new system can understand, and they fulfill the files of the acquired package.

Some conversion programs can be quite complex, because of the state of the data to be converted. It may be necessary to generate new coding from the original codes, or to create an algorithm to try to eliminate entries that do not fit under certain criteria. (This is done so that the company can start off with cleaner records in the new system, by avoiding the loading of obsolete or erroneous information.)

One good reason the company should take on the responsibility for running conversion programs is that its in-house personnel are intimately familiar with how the data are distributed in the current systems. This familiarity can facilitate one aspect of the problem.

The other aspect of the problem—how the software will work with the data—will depend on how much the software vendor concerned itself with investing to facilitate the preparation of the initial data for the new system. Some packages offer programs requiring that the client develop the *extraction* of the data from its current systems and format that data according to a particular predefined pattern. All of the rest of the process is automatic. In other words, these programs were developed to validate the data received and to update the package files, starting from the validated information.

Probably you have already realized that in the event that necessary company information is not contained in some system, the only alternative is to carry out the work of data entry and validation manually, in order to prepare the data to be processed in the company's new system.

For all of the reasons just mentioned, I always recommend to my clients that they start the process of the *initial load* as soon as possible during the package implementation project. As we have seen, this data needs to be available in the system even in the middle of the project. Many of the tasks to be executed soon thereafter can be performed better if the initial data is present. (For example, the system's end users' training must show how the package actually functions in normal day-to-day operations.)

It is unrealistic to imagine that all of the data required by the software can be converted. For every package there is certain unique information that cannot be brought in from other systems (because it does not exist in these systems). This information will have to be keyed in manually. With luck, the labor will not be significant and will be restricted to just a few tables or parameters.

The other issue involving programming is more delicate: the development of the interfaces. Interfaces provide a means of integrating older systems that will remain in place and the new package that is being implemented. As was stated previously, in today's world, it is fundamental to guarantee the integration of a company's data in order to avoid duplication and unnecessary additional work and to minimize costs. Unless the package, or packages, being acquired can substitute totally (with room left over) for the current systems—and this might be possible if the company were to select an integrated software package of a comprehensive scope (see Chapter 2)—it will be necessary for in-house specialists to develop programs that permit the exchange of information between the package and the systems that remain in place.

Interfaces are generally undesirable objects. They are complex, unique to each company, and, to a certain degree, they involve clumsy additions to the modern, state-of-the-art technology of a good new package. In many projects in which I have had the opportunity to work, interfaces have been one of the bottlenecks in the package implementation process. Nevertheless, I can state, as of the present date (1998), that interfaces are still an issue for most such projects, because of the absence of practical solutions to substitute, in on fell swoop, for all current systems. Systems with the widest scope take a great deal of time to implement (years, for some corporations) and require that interfaces be constructed, tested, and maintained for a certain time, although provisionally. Once again, knowledge of current systems that will interface with the package resides with in-house personnel. They must necessarily become involved in the development of such interface programs.

The topic of interfaces illustrates quite well the idea of the tripod mentioned earlier. The consultants determine the need for the interface and design how it should work. The company develops the interface, with the support of the package vendor, who will monitor, or even program, the package side of the interface. Once the interface is ready, the consultants test it and provide a procedure for activating the interface in the procedures manual they are preparing for the specific package implementation.

The Role of the Other Participants

In addition to the company personnel, the software vendor, and the consultants, who together comprise the troop that will put on the show, other players, from time to time, will enter the scene. They might participate at certain key junctures and add significant value to the work because of their specialties. We are referring to the hardware vendor, the database vendor, the network or telecommunications specialist, and, eventually, the vendor of development tools, as well. In summary, these are people or companies whose contribution is important because of the contracting company's need to train its informatics personnel, to configure the network, to fine-tune the database, to determine the minimum transmission speed, and because of a series of other issues that may arise as a function of how new the technology required to implement the package is in relation to the current data processing environment, as well as the practical experience of the company's informatics personnel.

We can expect that for the latest generation of software packages, which already take advantage of the most advanced characteristics of databases and operating systems available in the market, the use of a few hours (or a few days) of a specialist's time could be well worth the cost. In this event, consultants can also be of help. Usually they have some such specialists within their ranks, or they have developed alliances with companies or individuals who complement their services. We will return to this topic in Chapter 6.

Contracts: Which Clauses Are Important?

It may seem incredible, but just when all the issues and doubts seem to appear to have been resolved and the company's representatives have to put down on paper what has been agreed to by signing the products and services contracts, someone appears who will place a series of obstacles and concerns in the heads of all involved (I said all!). This is the company's lawyer or someone from its legal department.

How is the issue of contracts resolved? In general, the vendors and service providers already have a *standard contract,* (drafted by their lawyers or legal departments) that, in theory, should meet the general needs of the contracting company. This standard contract is analyzed by the contracting company's lawyers and, probably, questioned in certain regards. If reasonably conducted—not transferring all the responsibilities to the other side—this process can be healthy.

The standard contract, in the case of the software package, for example, should already contain clauses that clearly protect the contracting company against any complaint of inappropriate use of copyrights. That is to say, the software vendor guarantees that as the producer of the package it has the right to sell the product, or having been constituted the producer's legal representative, to distribute the system.

One point that always generates a certain amount of debate is whether the contracting company should have access to the source programs in order to guarantee processing continuity in the event that the package vendor is unable to honor its commitments, or the vendor company is subsequently sold or fails.

The sources and the design of the data model used in the software program constitute the software vendor's principal physical asset. It is here that the intelligence behind the product lies. The source program can be easily copied by anyone sufficiently competent to figure out the code, so it is unreasonable to think that the package vendor will be inclined to turn over this information to a client. Furthermore, exactly why should the company want this source code? To modify it? But by doing so, it would automatically lose one of the benefits it gains by acquiring the software package: the outsourcing of information systems maintenance. Once the source code has been altered without the vendor's authorization, or once the vendor has signed off on it, the vendor is no longer responsible for the compatibility of future versions of its system with the specific installation in question.

Remember that acquiring a software package is a process of partnership. The vendor was chosen, among other things, for being among the players believed to be the most likely to survive in this highly competitive technology market. Since no one is able to guarantee the future with absolute certainty, clauses are generally inserted in contracts to the effect that third parties (normally banks) will keep a copy of the source codes in their custody, and that they are authorized to turn these over to the contracting company if certain contractual conditions are met. Most package clients are satisfied with such a solution.

If the worst happens, that is, the vendor or the product disappear from the market, the contracting company's installation will not disappear with them. The package will continue to work, and, during a certain period, if necessary, the company can recruit the support of some of the vendor's professionals who, finding themselves suddenly out of work, can use their knowledge about the package to provide temporary services, or perhaps permanently join their former client's company.

Let's also remember our consultant friends, who know the package and are firmly committed to keeping the contracting company in good shape. They may—and should—be called in to discuss available alternatives and to provide immediate support to ensure process continuity. All of this is to say that if the implementation was well conducted, there will be sufficient time to define a continuity solution, one that permits the preservation of the investments and permits calm negotiation of an eventual substitution for the system.

It should be noted that during the last few years products and companies have, of course, disappeared. Software vendors have gone under because they are unable to maintain the investment volume necessary to survive in a continually growing market.

Therefore, the contract to be signed between the contracting company and the package vendor should contain, in addition to a clause about source programs, definitions of the following points:

- value of the software acquisition and the conditions of payment;
- a list of the documentation to be delivered with the package;
- the conditions for acquiring complementary modules in the future or for expanding the number of users granted permission to access the package;
- the cost of basic training for key users;

- the amount of annual maintenance fee (in general, a percentage of the acquisition price);

- the minimum period of obligatory maintenance (from one to five years);

- stipulation of the guaranteed receipt of new product versions and the criteria for making available these new versions;

- the conditions for use of vendor technical support (hot line, visits, remote support, response time, what is included in the annual maintenance fee, what must be paid in addition to this yearly fee, and how to deal with service expenses);

- rules and fees for customization services; and

- specific responsibilities assigned to the vendor over the course of the package implementation project.

Another important contract is the one to be signed with the consultants for the implementation services. What should the company be concerned about with respect to formalizing the consulting process? Compared to software packages, implementation services are of a more subjective nature. What the company wants is for the package to work, as it has been presented by the vendor's representatives and as documented in the manuals. What the company expects from the consultants it hires is that they will make the project succeed; that the implementation project will be executed within the established time period, according to the projected budget, that user satisfaction will be guaranteed; and that key users will be adequately prepared to operate the system and, thus, generate the expected benefits.

Because of the subjective nature of consulting services, and the fact that not all the actual conditions under which the project will be developed can be anticipated, it is vital that the consulting contract define criteria to be used to analyze situations where some doubt exists, without generating controversies (a task that is not always feasible).

The following points should be discussed with consultants:

- the team to be allocated to the project (a profile of each member, professional categories, part- or full-time commitment);

- fees and payment conditions;
- the project timetable;
- a summary of the methodology to be applied in the project;
- the scope of the work (one of the more complicated items, indicating what is included in the context of the project work and what is not);
- a list of project deliverables (reports, manuals, programs, etc.);
- the forms and methods of formal monitoring of project progress (the basis used for evaluating partial results), such as monitoring meetings and progress reports.

Often the consulting firm's proposal already covers most of these points and can be incorporated as an appendix and integral part of the service contract. Consequently, the actual contract itself can be substantially condensed, covering only the additional issues that require negotiation.

Common sense should be used insofar as allowing the definition of contractual clauses to become a major stumbling block to the start of the project. Remember, all parties should be exposed to some degree of risk, since this is to be a partnership. To strive for exaggerated protection tends to discourage the vendors and the consultants and, eventually it makes work on the project impossible.

The Role of the Integrator

In recent years some companies, upon contracting software implementation services, have sought to further limit their responsibilities in the implementation project by contracting with a single *system integration* firm. By doing so they avoid establishing individual contracts with the various vendors involved in projects of this nature.

Once the software package to be used by the company has been selected, the idea is to negotiate all project components—hardware, software, training, and implementation services—with one vendor who, in turn, will be held responsible for managing and paying all of the other parties involved

in the venture. This n
cover all products and
these financial resourc
lished contractually an

The advantage to th
management is simpli
pany will deal with onl
representative of this
components of service
integrator, company le
to deal with will dimir
the business will need
role of the integrator,
leaders in the manager

Some consulting firm
take on this role. But th
cal question to be decid
to provide system inte

Integration services, which al
the informatics service indust
and become a natural optio
plex and comprehensive
Regardless of who
ers within the com
successfully wi
that the imp
the outco

must be prepared to play this role by having strengths in the following areas:

- a methodology to manage the products and services to be integrated;
- partnerships with third parties to facilitate the process and the integration of the components;
- the legal support to appropriately exercise the function of integrator, a knowledge of the legal risks of such situations, and a clear understanding of and experience with the limits and responsibilities of its subcontractors;
- the capacity to deal with diverse and complex topics, such as equipment, networks, basic software and applications software, subcontracted labor, training infrastructure, graphic services, and so forth;
- the structure and knowledge to correctly administer the capital of third parties in the operation of the project.

eady represent an important segment of
ry, will probably continue to grow rapidly
n when a company decides to implement com-
software.

s responsible for project management, decision mak-
pany adopting the new software will still have to deal
h the issues presented in this book in order to guarantee
ementation work develops in a satisfactory manner, and that
ne brings the expected benefits.

5

Organizing the Implementation Project

Who within the Company Should Participate in the Project?

The most immediate response to the question of who should participate in the implementation project is probably *everyone*. If the software package being installed is an integrated system, as previously stated, everyone in the company must certainly participate, in one way or another. The functionality of a comprehensive integrated system, by definition, will extend to practically every sector of the company.

But there is no need to panic. The entire company need not be paralyzed for several months just to implement a new software package. But in its role as the owner of the project, as described in the previous chapter, the company will need a professional from each of its major departments to carry out a specific project function. Roles may be large or small, but each is equally fundamental for the implementation to be a success. Most important, all business functions having some relation to the future system must be represented appropriately in the project—from the executive level to the lowest level of operation—so that the company can count on the commitment of every sector involved and so that the true impact the package will have on each business function, once the system becomes operational, can be assessed. Later in this chapter, where we look at how to structure a project, we will explore this issue more thoroughly.

Meanwhile, let's examine the proposition that the implementation of a comprehensive and integrated system demands that directors, managers, supervisors, and administrative and operational personnel understand how the new information environment will work. They must realize what is to change in relation to current procedures, what additional facilities the new technology will place at the users' disposal, how to operate the system efficiently, as well as various other important aspects pertaining to installing a new work environment, one that is much more productive.

For the right level of participation to occur, a group of representatives selected from various sectors of the company will need to immerse themselves in the project on several levels. Some personnel will work full-time, developing tasks together with the consultants. Others, also assigned full-time, will coordinate work. Executive-level personnel, through the Executive Committee, will be responsible for monitoring the effort, making resources available, and making decisions that help keep the project on track. Still others will participate at special moments, such as during workshops and operational training.

One thing to bear in mind is that the participation of in-house personnel does not end once the software has been selected. On the contrary, it is exactly at this point that their participation must intensify. We will return to this issue again throughout the book. Guaranteeing that personnel continue to be engaged throughout the implementation of the project is extremely important, although everything in the company's daily operations will conspire against this happening. Here are some examples of impediments a company may encounter:

- preparation of the annual budget;
- monthly closing;
- reports to headquarters;
- other concurrent projects (total quality management, cost reduction, organizational climate, and so forth);
- special requests from the president or directors, due yesterday;
- alterations in legislation that must be evaluated; and so on and so forth.

Maintaining the company's focus on the implementation of the software package, which will ultimately provide multiple tangible benefits to company personnel, is part of the art of managing the constant, everyday struggle over scarce resources that every organization has to deal with to meet its obligations.

The genuine concern and commitment of top management to execute the project, as envisioned, is a key factor in gaining and maintaining the commitment of in-house personnel. Any shift in priorities at the top regarding the importance of the project can end up making the professionals assigned to the project wonder whether they are in the right place at the company. They may begin to question whether the project is being taken seriously by the organization's decision makers.

Who Should Be Assigned to the Project?

Every company needs people who make mistakes, are not afraid to err, and who learn from the mistakes.

—Bill Gates

To understand the question of who should be assigned to the project, let's briefly analyze what a project to implement a software package must represent to the company that decides to acquire it.

As a result of this project, new business processes will be instituted to take the place of current work patterns in the company's various sectors. A strong new concept of information integration will take effect, such that any data entered into the system from one sector will immediately affect all others that use that data. Very probably, the technology to be used will bring with it a series of new concepts and resources that must be mastered and correctly employed to optimize the processing power of the package. A complete new set of management information may be generated by the new system, and this, in turn, will create a new decision-making process, one probably more agile than the current process. Built into the functionality of the package will be new techniques of administration, new management and planning concepts, new control tools, and new ideas that must be absorbed and incorporated into the company's ways of conducting its business.

With this perspective, let's return to the question, Who should be assigned to the project? The response is easy: the best professionals within the company's ranks! The company's leaders will want to invest in these people and create opportunities for them to excel within the company so that their careers can evolve within the company.

Where are these people? In various places, in management positions, and in operational positions. Undoubtedly, these are the people who have no time for anything else, because their bosses and colleagues count on their intelligence and dedication to make things go as they should.

As a consultant, I always question the assignment to the project of "available" in-house personnel to the implementation project. How can anyone be "available" in these days? Availability in the present business world usually means that there is some limitation of capability, some accommodation, or, at the very least, that a person has been set aside by superiors or colleagues. A project that is going to require grappling with issues as complex as those we have been discussing thus far cannot use people with weak initiative, shallow dedication, and little enthusiasm; people who have difficulties in relationships or who lack experience. Implementing a software package is work for those who are able to fight like lions, those who see in the project a chance to gain visibility among peers and to earn new positions in the company (or even outside it).

Therefore, when faced with the decision regarding who is to work in the package implementation project, company leaders should be ready to bargain firmly for the recruitment of critical personnel. Invariably, the people selected are those whose responsibilities are impossible to interrupt, those for whom it would be difficult to find someone to keep things going in their absence. But the results are worth it. Using the best people is also a way of keeping consulting fees within budget. Obviously, in-house personnel who fail to produce what is expected must have their work complemented, or even taken over, by the professionals from the contracted consulting firm. The result: more hours, more costs.

As we shall see below, it is fundamental that the company designate a professional to manage the project, someone whose responsibility it will be to coordinate the activities of in-house personnel, to evaluate the consultants' work, and to serve as an intermediary between the executive and the operational level of the company during software implementation. This person should be someone in whom the company places its highest confidence, someone who is being considered for a leadership position, and someone who needs exposure and the opportunity to confirm his or her potential of eventually taking over from the business's current leaders.

How Many People Should Be Assigned to the Project?

Maintain your forces concentrated and in the best shape possible. This is the main idea. Anticipate everything as much as is possible.

—Karl von Clausewitz

How many people should be assigned? The answer depends totally on the nature of the software to be implemented, the technological environment that is to serve as the base for the system, and on the degree of responsibility the company intends to assume during the implementation work. No formula exists to calculate this number, and we can state that, in practice, each case is unique. Nevertheless, I will try to supply some basis for gauging the need, which, probably, the consultants will estimate anyway. Being responsible for doing the work, they will strive to obtain the level of support necessary to assure success.

Each major business process within the company—accounting, finance, sales, inventory control, human resources, production planning, distribution, and so forth (the classification of these processes will depend somewhat on the nature of the company's business)—each of these major processes must have at least one key user assigned to the project for a significant number of hours. Depending on the size of the company and on the diversity of the business in question (whether it produces different products or services, has geographic divisions, and so forth), it may be necessary to assign one person from every process area for each geographic division or product line.

It is also useful to assign to the project professionals from the informatics sector so that together with the departments' representatives, they can cover every aspect of the software. In general, the allocation of these people will be according to the natural modularization of the acquired software—financial, sales and marketing, maintenance and services, production, and so forth—with one informatics professional assigned to each module.

The informatics personnel are the people who, except for the in-house coordinator, will dedicate the most time to the project. They will be charged with mastering the product, understanding how the systems should work, and helping to prepare the entire company to place the new software into operation.

How Can the Project Be Structured?

Figure 5.1 describes, in an approximate manner, how the contracted consultants may suggest that the project be organized administratively so that the team can develop the tasks projected in the work schedule, and also so that management can monitor the whole software package implementation.

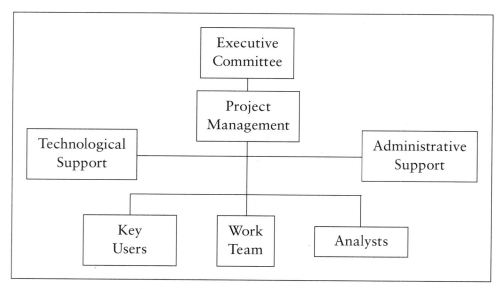

Figure 5.1   How the Project Can Be Structured

Let's analyze in more detail how the organizational structure of the project will work by examining the necessary division of work.

Executive Committee

This group is made up of representatives of the contracting company's top management (directors, the company's president, and other people who have decision-making power), the person with overall responsibility for the work of the contracted consultants (normally called the partner or director) and, eventually, someone from the executive level of the software vendor firm. The Executive Committee is responsible for evaluating the progress of the project, approving the intermediate and final results, providing the necessary resources to keep the work moving, according to the established timetable, and for making decisions when issues arise that might affect the defined scope or the estimated time and costs. Within the scope of its duties is renegotiating consulting fees and costs for services to be carried out by the package vendor (including training, customization).

Project management team

This team of two project managers is composed of the consulting professional who leads the field work (technical leadership) and a company representative named as in-house coordinator of the project (as indicated earlier in the chapter). These managers are responsible for conducting the scheduled work, administering the project (personnel, timetable, costs, expenses), communicating with company personnel who are to dedicate themselves part-time to the project (users, directors, third parties), and settling accounts with the Executive Committee on a regular basis so that the company's top management can appropriately monitor the evolution of the project, evaluate the preliminary results, and make the correct decisions that will establish continuity and achieve the goals of the project.

As has already been stated, the in-house coordinator appointed by the company should not limit himself or herself to executing or simply monitoring the tasks defined by the consultants. This person must also evaluate the quality and evolution of the consultants' work, discuss doubts with the leader of the consulting team (the manager), and ensure that company personnel involved in the project are adequately complying with their responsibilities. The in-house manager should see to it that all the knowledge necessary to operate the software package in the future will be absorbed gradually and consistently by every user to be involved in the processing of the new system.

Being assigned the role of manager should not be mistaken for being assigned to a project for the sole purpose of checking to see that things get done. Some package implementation projects have almost failed exactly because the company, through its project representatives, understood the manager's job as involving only verifying how things are going. The in-house coordinator must lead the company's personnel effectively so that everyone collaborates in the development work, dedicating themselves to doing the very best possible job and never losing sight of the project's objectives, which should motivate everything that occurs. Obviously, members of the Executive Committee must also concern themselves with this responsibility.

The in-house manager should bear in mind that, as the project develops, he or she needs to be increasingly prepared to present and discuss the various technical, functional, managerial, and political issues associated with the software implementation effort when anyone in the company requires an explanation. Such a positive and participatory attitude will confirm to company superiors the expectations they held when considering this person for the position.

Work Team

This team is composed of the people who will dirty their hands by actually carrying out each of the tasks set forth in the project work plan. These tasks range from extracting information from users to monitoring the start-up of processing under the new system. The people on the team should be professionals who, ideally, will dedicate full time to the project and concern themselves with successfully concluding each step planned in the project schedule. Doing this work well requires team spirit, a cooperative attitude, patience, persistence (as we shall see, the unforeseen *does* occur), and a great deal of confidence.

The work team normally includes the contracted consultants. These professionals should already understand the acquired software and, preferably, have had the opportunity to go through similar implementation experiences at other companies. It is reasonable to expect that the knowledge level with respect to the package will vary among the consultants. Nevertheless, taken together, the expertise of the consultants must be sufficient to guarantee satisfactory completion of the implementation process. For certain complex, integrated software packages, it is practically impossible to find a single professional who has mastered all of the functionality available in the package. In some cases, it is important to have on the project team people who are profoundly knowledgeable about the contracting company's field of business, or a specific aspect of that business, although these professionals may not be experts in working with the package, because the quality and success of the implementation effort will also depend on how the features of the software are used by the company. (As we shall see in Chapter 9, tables and parameters are critical items for good package implementation.)

The reason I do not list the contracting company's personnel as part of the work team, as illustrated in the diagram of the project's organization, is merely to facilitate the present explanation and description of responsibilities. I will outline the responsibilities of company personnel under the separate headings of "key users" and "analysts." Nonetheless, it is perfectly acceptable to design an organizational chart for the project that includes the company's personnel on the work team.

Key Users

The designation *key* users already indicates a series of characteristics. These people are the future users of the system, but, more than that, they are the ones who are to define how the system is to operate in all its detail. A key user is typically a company employee who possesses a certain autonomy in his or her field of activities. This person is seen as a natural leader of his or her colleagues, an opinion maker, a professional whose technical knowledge is respected by others. Consequently this person is a fundamental player when it comes to demonstrating to non-key users, who will also be future users of the system, that the changes the new software will bring to current processes will be of great benefit to the company and to its employees.

Key users will be the first to receive training on how to operate the software. They must know how the system works in order to evaluate the impact the software will have on the company's current business processes. They will also discuss with the consultants and the package vendor the level of customization the product will require in order to function appropriately in the company. Key users will help in testing such customization once it is ready, and they will approve the redefinition of procedures that become necessary in order to use the software correctly within the company.

In most implementation projects, key users actively participate in training other users when the package and procedures, duly adapted to the needs of the company, are ready for normal use.

Analysts

By *analysts* we are referring to professionals from the informatics sector of the company whose responsibility revolves around two principal roles.

First, starting from the premise that these people understand the current systems and business characteristics of the company, they can greatly facilitate the consultants' work of surveying and understanding the present situation. In-house analysts will develop (or coordinate the development of) programs to be used for data conversion, and they will help determine how to establish interfaces between the acquired package and the other systems that will remain in operation after the new software is installed. The active participation of the company's informatics professionals is vital to keep consulting fees within the planned parameters.

Second, these analysts, distributed and assigned so as to cover all functionality provided by the applications, must thoroughly understand how the package modules within their area of responsibility function, because later, when the package is up and running, they will provide user support.

Also, once the in-house analysts are trained in the ins and outs of the package they will be able to derive maximum benefit from the software, in terms of operational and managerial information. When future versions of the package become available, they may implement the new versions using in-house resources or contracting only limited assistance from consultants.

A cooperative environment with mutual trust between the company's analysts and the consulting firm's work team is a critical factor for satisfactory project development. In practice, this situation must be closely monitored by the Project Management Team and by the Executive Committee. Experience has demonstrated that such an ideal working relationship is not established naturally. There may exist a certain feeling among some of the employees that the consultants and packages are coming "to invade our space," a space that was, for years, almost totally the domain of the MIS sector, because the technology market did not offer many really competitive solutions. The situation has changed radically since then. It is vital that the company's informatics professionals understand the new role and focus reserved for the MIS sectors of companies. Today their efforts will be directed more toward supporting user operations instead of creating highly personalized (and expensive) solutions to practically any problem or need the functional sectors of the company deemed necessary to conducting their work. In the past these practices generated a notorious backlog of user requests, generally months or years long. (For this very reason, in some places, the backlog was nicknamed the "back-long.")

To monitor the new computing environment, appropriate in-house analysts need to be assigned to the project, the company's objectives for the project need to be made clear to these people from the start, what is to be expected from the participation of informatics personnel needs to be communicated, and the relationships that develop between personnel from both entities (particularly analysts within the company and members from the consulting firm) need to be watched closely. Consultants have their own techniques for checking out the terrain upon which they will tread, and they can usually anticipate problems and avoid them, either by speaking openly with the professional who demonstrates a certain antipathy, or by taking the problem to the project's Executive Committee.

Technological Support

The data processing environments being adopted by companies to support applications and systems to reduce administrative costs and to provide more accessible and timely information are, generally speaking, simple to use—once they are in place and working. But such environments are complex in terms of facility stabilization and monitoring. Everything has to work in perfect harmony: the network, the computers, the database, the applications. Some issues that are involved are performance (the speed with which processing occurs), data backup and recovery, the fine-tuning of the database, equipment configuration, access authorizations, and various other technical aspects that must be handled by people with the right technical skills. These specialists are responsible for adjusting the environment so that the user experiences a secure, fast, and reliable system.

Being able to adjust the environment is important because the resulting processing environment will have a direct impact on users' satisfaction with the new software solution. It does no good to implement the world's best software system if its response time is poor, or if data suddenly disappears without explanation. Users will reject the software and the solution will lose credibility.

In the recent past, technological support for implementation projects was a part-time activity, carried out by vendor and company technicians (when available), consultants, or by third parties (firms or freelancers specialized in this type of support). Nowadays this activity has become more and more critical to project success, because of the increasing complexity of systems, supplier diversity, and because the processing capacity has to be distributed among hundreds of user sites that are geographically dispersed. Currently it is advisable to plan for technical support to be a full-time activity; it is reasonable to see the technical infrastructure tasks as another project that will coincide and interact with the software implementation project.

The project's work plan must allow for the participation of technical staff at appropriate times, and Project Management must guarantee that technical support will be activated in the event that technical problems arise during the development of the project.

Administrative Support

Professionals involved in a project of a certain complexity and duration need to have their lives made easier so that they can concentrate the greatest part of their time on the planned activities. Only in this manner will the original objectives be achieved. What does making life easier for these professionals mean? Various things. Making available a work space devoted exclusively to the project, with tables, chairs, telephones, book shelves, filing cabinets, and, without a doubt, microcomputers loaded with word processors, electronic worksheets, presentation software, and project management software. It also means making the process of copying documents, sending and receiving faxes or data (via modem) easy, by assigning an assistant (even if shared) to set up meetings, receive messages, and deal with the internal bureaucracy of the company. A support person can make arrangements for travel and lodging when the project involves transferring people from other locations, and, depending on the location of the work site, making arrangements to feed outside personnel during their time on the project and arranging for parking spaces for these professionals.

It is clear that the administrative support function does not necessarily have to be carried out by a fixed group of people; the important thing is that the company needs to acknowledge and understand the needs of a project of this nature and prepare itself to meet these needs in a satisfactory manner, thus avoiding administrative conflicts that could interfere with the progress of the work.

Where Should the Project Team Work?

It is important that the project be allotted its own space where its assigned professionals can meet and work. Designating a room to accommodate only the contracted consultants, while maintaining the company's personnel at their original work locations, is not a good solution to promote the desired productivity. A person assigned to the project needs to feel he or she is an integral part of the work and a member of a team, not imagine that he or she will only be largely dedicated to the effort, but, in reality, the day-to-day activities will also continue as always.

A work site organized according to the preferences of the participants will help create an identity and a feeling of belonging for team members, which is basic to generating and maintaining the team spirit and joint collaboration that will produce results.

6

Implementation Methodology: A General Overview

What Does a Software Implementation Project Look Like?

Time is unfaithful for those who abuse it.
—Metastásio

When one talks about methodologies of systems, a curious thing happens. At first glance all the methodologies look very much alike. For example, many terms and names are common to all of them. But after talking with consultants one begins to see that certain important differences exist when it comes to methodologies. Every consulting firm tries to demonstrate its uniqueness for dealing with the implementation of packages or systems; every contracting company tries to identify what appears to be the most appropriate way to develop a business solution.

The bottom line of this apparent difficulty—similar methodologies and a single problem to resolve (to implement systems)—is that, to compare the different approaches, the contracting company must pay attention to small details. (By the way, *approaches* is perhaps a better word than *methodology* to define the work of consultants.) The differences, in this case, are in the little things: the content of a particular overhead transparency, a comment made by one of the members of the consulting team during a presentation, and, principally, the practical demonstration that the consultants really have dealt with the particular software in question.

If the consulting firm has practical experience, the methodology (or approach) for attacking the package implementation project will have been adapted to include tasks or activities specially tailored to the specific application being analyzed. This may be apparent in one or more of the following aspects of the project: training, master files definition, tables and parameters (modeling), initial load plan and test plan, the definition of procedures and customization, the development of interfaces, the adjustment of the processing environment, the definition of accesses and permission, and so forth. The list is inexhaustible, but these are some of the aspects that are most subject to comparison. If the differences between consultants are not evident during presentations, do not hesitate to ask!

This said, let's return to the overview of the project and describe a generic approach that can be used as a basis for judging the various service proposals presented by consultants. Figure 6.1 illustrates this overview. In Chapters 8, 9, 10, and 11 we will analyze in detail all of the phases of software package implementation process. In the meantime, let's establish that, generally, (as demonstrated in Figure 6.1) the work can be organized into four principal phases. Each produces an intermediate result that can be evaluated, adjusted, and then approved, so that the project team can continue on with the certainty that the work is evolving satisfactorily toward the project's defined objectives. The four principal phases are described as follows:

Phase 1

In Phase 1 the goal of those carrying out the project is to establish the foundation that permits the software package to be implemented in the

Phase 1	Understanding the problem
Phase 2	Defining the solutions
Phase 3	Putting hands to the task
Phase 4	Making it happen

Figure 6.1   Overview of the Project

best manner possible. It is necessary to understand the kind of business the company conducts and how the package will fit with the business's processes. Decision makers and project team members who will carry out this phase of the project need to determine the characteristics of the current systems and what part of them will be preserved in the new information processing environment; arrange for basic training for the key users and analysts who will participate in the project; delineate any peculiarities of the company that may generate the need for customizing the software; and determine how the stored data will be migrated to the new systems in order to plan the most effective way to do this.

Phase 2

The second is the most critical phase because during its development all concepts associated with the operation of the software package will be defined. The project team will conduct simulations of the application processing to identify differences between the present work processes and the new work environment that will come into being once the software is fully implemented. All basic definitions of information and data (modeling)—master files, tables and parameters—will be made. The degree to which the company will have to adapt to the package is established, and vice versa (customizations are defined). The interfaces between the package and the systems that will remain will be studied and planned. In summary, it is possible during this phase to create a prototype (for this reason, this phase is sometimes called *prototyping*) or model of the future operations of the system.

Phase 3

If Phase 2 is the most critical, Phase 3 is the most difficult. It is in this phase that the project schedule may flounder. In the previous phases the project team was concerned with defining and detailing. This involved a lot of paperwork, and, as someone once said who, no doubt, had a lot of experience in implementing something planned by others, "Anything is possible on paper." In Phase 3 the objective is to do the work. The project team will load the initial data; develop, test, and place the customization into operation;

develop and test the interfaces and place them into operation; document the new procedures associated with the system; test the new work environment; and train a multitude of new users.

Phase 4

To arrive at Phase 4—the moment at which the software will start to be used—is synonymous with being close to success. There is no guarantee of success, because this project phase may still hold surprises, as we shall see in Chapter 11. The focus here is on making the system "happen." The software is usually run in parallel with the current systems for a time. In this phase the project team will provide support to users who are still insecure in the new work environment; be ready to make final adjustments that become necessary; and, finally, release the system for normal use, giving the order to pull the plug on the current systems. Wow! This is the moment of greatest anxiety, but it also carries a sense of great accomplishment for all. For the project team, even more than the sense of fulfilling their duty is the feeling of having created something new and useful that will benefit the company and its personnel, and to have contributed toward maintaining the company's competitiveness in an increasingly demanding market, one in which reinventing business processes is, above all, a question of survival.

What Results Can the Company Expect?

The bad thing about making intelligent suggestions is that you run the risk of having to carry them out.

—Oscar Wilde

As we will see in Chapter 8, Phase 1 of the implementation project includes tasks of project organization, to guarantee that everything is developed satisfactorily. Determining the expectations of company leaders and personnel in terms of project results is normally one of the tasks that falls within this phase. Members of the project team might interview key personnel, those who have decided that the investment must be made and, thus, expect that this investment will bring a certain form of return. This certain form of return is what needs to be understood by the group that will develop the project.

We place this question first because it merits special treatment. The objective of the software package implementation project is not simply to make the package work in the company as it (the package) was designed, but rather to make it work to produce the results that the project's investors imagined when they concluded that buying this software package was a viable and necessary investment. This issue is not so simple as it may seem, because during the process of evaluating and selecting the package and, subsequently, during the implementation of the project, the objectives envisioned by the company's executives may not have always been clear or comprehensively examined. The issue becomes even more complex if these executives did not actively participate in the purchasing process but delegated the decision to a more technical group of professionals.

Not only do the expectations of company leaders and personnel with respect to the project need to be understood, but they need to be calibrated before things start to happen. Those conducting the implementation project (the consultants and the in-house personnel) need to demonstrate what the company can expect as a result of the work, what is *not* possible, and also what is *not* expected but will be desired, because it will happen with the new system (this is the good news, the agreeable surprise!)

It is incredible how many consultants relegate the question of company expectations to second place and, consequently, end up with egg on their faces when the project is at a well-advanced stage and the client company brings up concerns about the outcome of the project. At this point any significant shift in course would mean considerable delays, reworking, and many hours that were not planned. At this juncture, certain situations can occur, all of them embarrassing: misunderstandings with the client (the company) that can result in aftershocks, regardless of the solution devised for addressing the problem; a drastic reduction in the profitability of the project for the consulting firm, or even an actual loss because additional hours have to be invested and the company refuses to pay extra; delays in the completion of tasks—one of the plagues of informatics services—they seem never to finish by the established deadline; and doubts among in-house personnel regarding the actual possibilities for project success that, alone, already diminish the chance of success. Positive thoughts, confident attitudes—these are the fundamental ingredients for achieving the planned objectives.

The discussion, understanding, adjustment, and documentation of the company's expectations regarding the results of the project can represent the difference between success and failure. Therefore, arriving at an understanding demands attention from those who are to conduct the work, the consultants, as well as those who are paying for it, the company's shareholders. Therefore, during the period when services are initially being contracted, verification of the extent to which the candidates for the contract understand the company's expectations may help the company's decision makers to choose among the various proposals made to get the job.

Carrying out this task sufficiently does not guarantee that everything will go marvelously, but it certainly establishes a basis for discussing problems that may arise along the way among all those involved. It fosters an environment of mutual understanding, one in which the project's success is always safeguarded as the company searches for the best solution.

Is the Appropriate Technological Environment Available?

Since the decision to acquire and implement a software package is generally accompanied by a substitution or an expansion on the current data processing environment, company decision makers need to realize that very early in the project they will need to consider creating a new environment that will support the operation of the new system.

As has already been stated, buying a new system usually means acquiring the new equipment and database software, and sometimes installing a fiber optic communication infrastructure, making communication by satellite viable, as well as installing the innumerable vital physical and logical instruments that are prerequisites for operating the acquired package. Frequently, many of these setups and devices are not available for immediate use in the company (that is, there is a minimal waiting period before they will become available), and the installation of some, for example, satellite communications, may even depend on government authorization.

Worse still, these days all the various technology vendors do not work in an integrated fashion. That is to say, they develop their products in isolation from one another based on their own concepts and unilateral assumptions, and, subsequently, as use indicates the need for improvements, they continually modify these products so that the environment purchased by their clients is effectively integrated, and free of failures. This is the reason that many people look back nostalgically on the golden age of the mainframe, when all components were supplied by a single firm.

If the decision to alter the technological environment actually preceded the decision to acquire the package, and an infrastructure close to that required to operate the new system already exists, fine, because any technical work that remains to be done probably will not significantly affect the implementation project timetable. But usually this is not the case. For most companies, the decision to acquire a package sets off a substitution process in the technological environment. The establishing of this new environment, normally carried out by informatics personnel within the company, must be closely monitored to avoid any circumstances that would delay having the system up and running by the required date.

The software package implementation will require using the new data processing environment right from the start, so that analysts and key users can be trained in the final processing environment. It is important that the first contact these people have with the application makes the best possible impression, because any misgivings regarding system performance, ease of use, or the stability of the processing environment will generate doubts about the new setup. In-house analysts and users may then assume defensive positions and criticize the process, instead of acting as facilitators and being responsible for its success. You can be sure that at the slightest sign of possible failure, all will beat a strategic retreat.

For all of these reasons, the company must not attempt to postpone disbursements by pushing back delivery of the final equipment for "later in the project, when it is really necessary." The idea that it is possible to work in an environment that is limited in terms of processing capacity during the first months of the implementation is an incorrect one. Obviously, it is not necessary to set up the entire network—all the workstations for when the package is fully operational—but the training, simulation, and testing environment must be as close as possible to the final processing environment, so that users can understand what their future work environment will really be like. This is necessary because there should be no limitations on the work of the professionals responsible for the project. By being able to work in the definitive environment from the start, they can better administer the adjustment process that will come after the installation of software in the new environment. The simulations and tests to be conducted will indicate where adjustments are needed, and thereby the company avoids having personnel make alarming discoveries in more delicate moments, for example, when they are in training.

Nowadays it is becoming more and more difficult to determine what is the most appropriate configuration to be installed as the system infrastructure. The diversity and quantity of the available components and the absolute need to integrate every piece of hardware and software makes the task very complex. Good performance, as was said before, is vital to make the user believe the software solution can be useful. It is recommended that the company's technical personnel team up with the software vendor and the consultants so that together they can produce a document describing the current and the proposed technological infrastructure. This commitment from all the participants will help produce a better analysis and also assure that none of the parties will try to blame the network and equipment configuration when things are not going as expected with the new setup.

My recommendation, therefore, is that as soon as possible, and before starting the package implementation work, the informatics sector of the company develop the contacts, solicit the bids, and determine the vendors who will supply the components of the new data processing environment. The document described above establishes a common list of requirements to be met by the vendors offering the components of the infrastructure. These vendors should be informed of the company's expectations in terms of delivery deadlines and facility support, so that they can make a realistic commitment to meeting these expectations from the start.

It is important to remember that to support this new technological environment, various professionals from the company's informatics personnel must be trained by the hardware vendors to qualify on the new hardware and software resources. The company also needs to consider the possibility of recruiting new staff experienced in this new technological environment, in order to shorten the company's learning curve for mastering the new technology.

Some companies have gone even further in the process of getting the new data processing environment up and running. To guarantee that energies and efforts are concentrated on the new technology, and to really demonstrate that the old systems and equipment will disappear, these companies have signed outsourcing contracts for their current processing environments (in general, composed of mainframes). Then they physically removed these systems and equipment from headquarters and even transferred some nonrecyclable professionals to the firm contracted to do the outsourcing work.

The new technology environment is a fundamental resource for implementing the acquired software package. Special attention must be paid to getting the setup just right so that the company avoids the situation where the technical environment becomes the limiting element in the implementation effort.

Should the Company Take Advantage of the Situation and Engage in Reengineering?

Whether or not it is advisable to reengineer the company when implementing a new software system is debatable. Some specialists say that a company cannot improve its internal processes just by installing a new software project. They maintain that implementing an important system without first examining the current processes and eliminating inefficiencies is a dubious proposition. Any existing inefficiencies have probably accumulated through years or decades of company culture, the company's history of success, in-house bureaucracy, current systems, the way its executives think, and because assumptions have never been challenged. Thus under the best of circumstances, simply implementing a new system in an attempt to improve businesses processes would lead to the underutilization of the potential the package offers.

But others maintain that there are software packages in today's market that are designed based on an analysis of what is conventionally called *best practices,* that is, the best ways of conducting a business function. They would argue that successfully implementing such a system, with the support of the company's leaders, already guarantees a natural revision of the company's current processes. Business processes are modified so that the new system can be used appropriately, and, better yet, the company does not need to officially announce that it is carrying out reengineering.

There is no absolute right or wrong approach, but there are conditions and situations that must be analyzed and clearly reported so that the company's top management can make a conscious decision while recognizing the consequences of its choices. Let's explore some possible conditions and situations in order to understand what is being considered in these decision processes.

In the first place, most companies have already conducted some type of reengineering. This business strategy has been brought on by a redefinition of markets, the need for scale economies, a decrease in profit margins, globalization, and a series of other well-defined and well-known conditions and circumstances. In practice, such reengineering has resulted in deep cuts in personnel costs and the firing of hundreds or thousands of employees at all levels of companies. The trauma caused by business restructuring, company mergers, the selling of divisions that contributed insufficiently to profits or in other ways has been of such an order that today the very use of the term *reengineering* has fallen into disfavor. I know of various companies that are careful when starting any review or revision to avoid damaging the morale of those who will be affected.

Therefore, the company's recent history is one condition to be analyzed: Is it worthwhile, or even necessary, to revise one or several business functions in order to optimize the operation of the future system?

As has been mentioned previously, many companies have decided to change their information systems environment because of the cost/benefit relationship made possible by many new software systems. It is common for company executives to discover that the company is spending five, ten, fifteen, twenty, or even forty million dollars a year on informatics, only to learn that the company's management information department basically depends on a few spreadsheets prepared on microcomputers by a tiny group of heroes who spend nights and weekends to produce the data that is the basis for analyzing the business. For the moment, the urgency of implementing new systems to end this situation may place the problem of improving the processes on the back burner. What is important is to get away from the wasteful practice.

In contrast, there is the company that views the new software package exclusively as a "tool for change." The company really intends to start a reengineering process, of a scope envisioned by its fomenters: The company will not limit itself to simply cutting costs; it will study how it can increase market share, introduce new products and services to increase revenues and earn decent profits. It is difficult to imagine a review of processes that is not accompanied by a technological solution to make the new ideas of efficiency and effectiveness feasible. In this situation the package is going to play a bigger role than just substituting for current systems; it will make it possible for the new processes to work as envisioned. In this situation, when decision makers are preparing a list of requirements the software package must meet, the restructuring of processes is one of the fundamental aims.

Generally, it is recommended that the project to implement a comprehensive and integrated system be preceded by an exercise to evaluate the company's management model. To do this, decision makers need to diagnose the basic issues that lead to the need for reengineering processes. Some aspects that are considered are centralization versus decentralization of administration; the feasibility of applying the ABC concept (activity-based costing) to manage the business's costs; the development of client and supplier relationships; the integration of the company's sales and marketing sector with its production sector; a review of the planning process; an introduction of the concepts of MRP II (material requirements planning) or enterprise resource planning (ERP) and other points. Once analyzed and discussed, these considerations may lead company decision makers to the conclusion that the company needs to prepare itself better in several specific business functions, or to consider that the project to implement an acquired software package should encompass a more thorough review of processes in certain business functions.

After evaluating the company's management model, decision makers can determine with greater precision what the next step for the company should be in its initiative to create a more productive, effective, and competitive work environment. The result of this effort will be an action plan containing very concrete objectives, in terms of the needs for restructuring or adapting the company's business functions. Either these objectives will be achieved through the installation of the newly acquired software alone, or they will require carrying out additional activities, in a manner that is consistent with the system's implementation timetable, in order to maximize project results.

In summary, companies cannot ignore the question of reengineering because, one way or another, it will be present in the implementation process. But it is fundamental to define the correct dosage that is required, in function of the objectives to be reached, and, above all, it is indispensable to know where the company wishes to go, when, and at what speed.

It Is Not Going to Be a Bed of Roses

The world belongs to the optimists. The pessimists are mere spectators.
—Eisenhower

The following are the typical phases people experience in the course of working on implementation projects:

- enthusiasm,
- concern,
- panic,
- search for the guilty,

- seeing the light at the end of the tunnel,
- the experience of results and success, and
- praise for those who didn't participate,

In my experience as a consultant, I have often been confronted by a very interesting client observation. When the negotiation for the job is well along and the decision in favor of my service proposal is practically official, some executives comment: "We're contracting with your firm because we want to be sure that we won't have any problems on this project!" (I presume that the contracting company is making a distinction between my firm and firms with lesser experience, that are less expensive, or that have no background in or reputation for implementing large and complex projects.) Faced with this comment, I answer in the following manner: "You are contracting my firm, among other things, because *a project like this most certainly will have problems.*" This is one of the reasons that a consulting firm made up of experienced professionals, possessing an appropriate methodology, and an international support network, or a firm that has a lot to lose if the project fails, presents benefits and added value that justify the proposed fees and make the firm worthy of the client's confidence.

Make no mistake: A project of this magnitude, involving issues as diverse as changes in technology, changes in business processes, the mobilization of hundreds of people, reliance on third parties, results that evolve over time and not immediately, competition with the day-to-day activities of the company, and pressure to meet deadlines and budgeted costs *will have problems.* There will be technical problems, political problems, conceptual disagreements, problems of a personal nature, moments of depression, discoveries of little things that no one had thought about before, moments of frenetic enthusiasm (nothing in excess is good), in summary, things and more little things that require prevention or rapid reaction, a spirit of fraternity, loyalty to the initially established objectives, the ability to see challenges where the weak or the reactionaries see only obstacles.

Figure 6.2 illustrates something interesting. The graph shows how people usually behave in projects of this nature. It is revealing to verify that

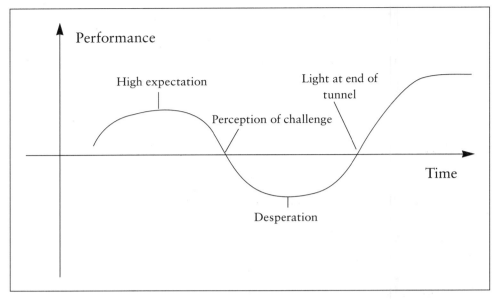

Figure 6.2   How People Behave

good moments and bad moments alternate. Knowing about things like this, how they happen and why they happen, represents incomparable experience in working for the project to succeed. It is of fundamental importance that company leaders and key personnel understand the shape of the project's "attitude" wave so that they can free themselves from false expectations. That way the project can continue to receive the vital support of top management and move onward toward the established objectives. It is the obligation of whoever is conducting the work to adequately present to the right people, just as soon as possible, issues that must be dealt with because they will have an impact on the outcome of the project. This is not always easy, because sometimes the problem involves individuals, and it is always traumatic to place a professional in check. But it is better to briefly embarrass someone than to suffer the consequences of inaction or of an incorrect action.

Everyone's objective, that of the consultants and of the company's personnel, must be to transform the curve in Figure 6.2 into an ascending curve, right from the start of the project. For this, team members need to discuss all issues with a maximum of openness (without getting personal). They need to plan what is to be done in detail, work realistically, document important decisions, cooperate whenever something unexpected occurs, and, first and foremost, always act positively, remembering that important things are before them to be conquered and that everyone will benefit if the venture succeeds.

It is worthwhile mentioning a phrase, one of the lessons in life variety, that applies well to the discussion at hand: "To avoid stress, two rules must be followed: (1) Do not concern yourself with small things; (2) everything is a small thing."

7

Evaluating and Monitoring the Development of the Implementation Project

Monitoring and Evaluating Project Development

A plan that cannot be changed isn't any good.

—Publius Syrus

When we described the role of the Executive Committee, we mentioned this group's responsibility to evaluate project progress. But how is this done? How can the company establish an information base to determine whether the work is being developed as anticipated? Whether the quality of the intermediate results is satisfactory?

In the first place, it is fundamental that the company—represented by the directors and managers chosen to participate on the project's Executive Committee—be aware that their role as owners of the project requires that they continually verify that intermediate work results are satisfactory and that the credibility of the professionals (both those in-house and those hired from outside the company) that are conducting the activities is maintained.

Although their attitude with respect to the evolution of the project must, in principle, be a positive one (company decision makers have, after all, proceeded very carefully to reach this point), during project monitoring meetings members of the Executive Committee must receive data that induce them to maintain confidence in the process. No, this does not mean that they should get only good news (remember, it's not going to be a bed of roses), but the good news, or the problems, must be presented in such a way that the Executive Committee gets the sense that the project is under control and that, with or without modifying the initial estimates, the project will continue to develop steadily and will meet the company's primary business objectives in the end.

How Is the Work Monitored?

Persistent work overcomes all.

—Virgil

In just about every chapter an important component of the management process for a software package implementation project has been mentioned—the work plan. It is a detailing of all of the activities to be undertaken in the course of the project.

Above all else, it is important that everyone involved in the project be aware that such a plan exists. Although it might be less than perfect, it is better than no plan at all. One cannot evaluate the progress of a complex project without comparing the intermediate results with those that were originally anticipated, or the costs that have been budgeted. Monitoring based on a feeling—or on the fact that the technical person in charge has had widespread experience working on similar projects—cannot be condemned offhand as inappropriate, yet such an approach does introduce a degree of risk into the project that is unacceptable in an overwhelming number of cases. Remember, we are talking about projects that involve significant sums of money and have business objectives with enormous impact on the company.

The work plan lays the basis for tracking the project. It covers numerous persons, many hours of labor, and a great deal of activities. Ideally, such a work plan is built with the help of software tools (known as project management systems), that permit one to focus on planned activities from various perspectives: the chronological sequence or timetable, specific activities and who is responsible for them, the prerequisites for carrying out particular activities, or a PERT chart of the activities (a graphical presentation of the interrelationship of activities, start dates and end dates, and the number of hours to be applied to each activity). Preparing the work plan using a tool of this type helps produce a high-quality project plan, with which team members can verify the consistency of the inserted data and time frames and see a graphical depiction of preliminary results. Once the project has started, the project file can be regularly updated with real-life data (the actual start and completion dates of activities, the actual time dedicated to each activity). The project management software can generate comparisons between actual and planned completion dates for analysis by those responsible for the project. Figure 7.1 presents a possible format for a software implementation project's work plan.

Phase	Stage	Task	Description	Responsible Party	Start Date	End Date	Execution Time (hours)
1	—	—	Phase 1	—	—	—	—
—	1	—	Present Situation	—	—	—	—
—	—	1.1	Identify Key Personnel	SL	4/10	4/10	4
—	—	1.2	Prepare Interviews	SL, PB	4/10	4/12	36
—	—	1.3	Conduct Interviews	SL, PB	4/13	4/19	80

Figure 7.1   Project Xxxxx—Work Plan

Assumptions: The Pillars of the Work Plan

Not knowing it was impossible, he went ahead and did it.
—Jean Cocteau

The basis for project planning is formed by what can be termed *assumptions*. These are the truths, assumed by everyone involved before the work starts, or they are the agreements among the parties—the company, the consultants, and the package vendor—that determine the environment in which the project is developed. To make the concept more clear, here are a few practical examples:

- The implementation of a particular software package assumes the availability of a new computer at a certain point in the projected timetable. The work plan prepared by the consultants dictates, for example, that the company acquires an interim machine (having the minimum capacity required) at the start of work activities so that the training of key users will not be delayed, and it stipulates that the definitive equipment needs to be installed by a certain later date. The project timetable, therefore, will depend on fulfillment of these tasks and their underlying assumptions.

- The selected package probably allows its database to be structured using one, among various, related database options. The company decides upon a database for which no relevant use in the market has been developed. That is to say, certain aspects, such as performance, bugs, or even the quality of the specific programming still need to be adjusted by the package vendor. This work might eventually affect the project timetable. In this case, it is assumed that a certain amount of time will be set aside for pioneering the technology, and this time must be sufficient to make the adjustments that need to be made. Or the premise could be a more optimistic one, based on the expectation that all will go well, that the results achieved are equivalent to those obtained with other databases in common usage.

- The work plan determines that company personnel will be totally responsible for various important activities. Thus a premise was adopted that certain in-house professionals can effectively dedicate themselves at the planned level of intensity, so that these activities can be carried out within the established time frame.

- In order for the selected software package to start running by a particular date, there is the premise that an internal system under development by company analysts and programmers (which will be vital to generate the basic information for processing data with the new software package) will be tested and ready in time to be integrated into the software implementation project.

It must be clear that a good work plan cannot be created on the basis of ideals, either pessimistic or optimistic, or simply based on previous experience. (There is no such thing as two identical projects.) A good work plan is one that, besides appropriately detailing the necessary activities, is based on assumptions that reflect factors of chief importance for the specific project and the company.

Experienced consultants try to develop their planning starting from a basic model or standard work plan for implementing a specific software package. Next they modify this initial plan, incorporating, detailing, or eliminating tasks according to the needs they detect during the information-gathering phase at the contracting company, as well as their understanding of the expectations held by the business's key personnel regarding anticipated project results.

The consultants then consider the time to be dedicated to each task and the background of the professional(s) who will carry out these tasks. During Phase 1 of the project, once the work plan has been detailed, the person responsible for planning can take into account the people to be assigned. Starting from this scenario, it is possible to define the start dates and completion dates for each task, as well as the assumptions upon which such dates are based.

It is important to realize that everything described thus far does not happen in a purely sequential fashion, as may appear at first glance. Instead, planning activities develop interactively, starting back at the time when the service proposal is being drafted and extending up to the moment when the work plan is presented to the Executive Committee for final approval.

In summary, a great deal of dialogue occurs along the way to define acceptable assumptions, execution times for tasks to be carried out by the company's personnel and outside consultants, and adjustment of the measurements—formal or otherwise—associated with monitoring the implementation project. Consultants need to fit their detailed plan into the more generic plan they have presented in the service proposal. The contracting company has already bought the block of time and paid the cost of the project, so if this turns out not to look possible, the company will need to renegotiate time frames, or fees, even before the project starts. (This situation frequently occurs after many months have already gone by since the date of first contact and the start of the project.)

Monitoring the Project

The first question is: With what frequency do company decision makers need to check on the progress of the project—weekly, biweekly, monthly, or quarterly? If the company has really assigned its best personnel to the job, as described in the previous chapters, there will already be a natural monitoring of the project's daily activities. The company professional assigned to serve as project manager, in his or her role as co-administrator of the work, occupies an ideal position to evaluate how things are going.

But, returning to the original question, for a project that is measured in many months, which is typically the case when a company is implementing integrated software packages, it is advisable that the Executive Committee meet to review progress on a monthly basis. This is because, for a project of this size, several weeks—four or five—are needed for a particular level of progress to be achieved. But at certain times during the project, for example, during the final stages, when the software starts to be used by the end users, it may be necessary to convene meetings more frequently to discuss specific issues that arise.

What sort of information should be presented in meetings held to track the progress of the project? To answer this question, let's analyze the project managers' objectives in convening such meetings:

1. to brief the Executive Committee in a clear manner regarding the project status to date;

2. to resolve issues that affect the work and that require a decision by the company's top management; and

3. to maintain the company's commitment to the project and to its objectives.

The meeting, which is normally conducted by the project managers (one from the consulting firm and the other from the company), might start off with a settling up of accounts. Together with the Executive Committee the project managers examine where the project is, how this compares with the initial forecast, or why the work is behind—or ahead—in relation to the timetable, what the team already has to show, and how the participation of company personnel has gone. The cards are laid on the table for certain project team members who have made valuable contributions, and those who are rowing against the course are skewered. In summary, the key decision makers deal with anything and everything that those managing the project may rightfully present to make the project's current status clear and understandable to all Executive Committee members.

Since this meeting with the Executive Committee is essentially a managerial meeting, it is important for the project managers to prepare a presentation that describes the situation at a level of detail appropriate to the audience. Very technical topics must be condensed; the excessive use of technical terms—bits and bytes jargon—will make many present feel they are being victimized by obfuscation. It is important for everyone to keep in mind the assumptions that organized the work and the objectives that the company set out to accomplish through the project. (After several months, people tend to forget how everything got started.)

It is suggested that the material used in this presentation should also serve to document the status of the project for the date in question, because in order to track progress at future meetings, it may become necessary to recall issues presented at some prior time, so as to explain why the evolution of the work has taken a particular route.

The second objective of the meeting—addressing issues that involve decisions from the company's top management—is more delicate. Such decisions will not necessarily need to be made at every meeting, but when they do have to be made, the meeting requires careful preparation. It falls on the project managers to analyze alternative solutions, their advantages, disadvantages, and consequences and present these to the committee. They must also assume a position with respect to what alternative they deem to be the most appropriate. A pro-active attitude is vital so that members of the Executive Committee will feel secure about making decisions at the speed required by the project.

Some issues that will need to be addressed might be, for example, that an initial assumption has failed to be met, and the company will have to revise the timetable; a key person assigned to the project has been reassigned to another job and a substitute must be found; the level of performance the system reached during the initial tests requires expanding the hardware capacity; it has become necessary to limit the amount of customization that can be done so as to keep to the timetable. There is no way to anticipate everything that may occur; but it is necessary for project managers to anticipate roadblocks as much as possible so that the project can be kept under control.

Generally, members of the Executive Committee are not going to appreciate being snookered. The project's managers must avoid the practice of presenting to the committee only problems that have become critical. An attempt to cover up problems almost always leads to a loss of credibility. The best approach is prevention; that means planning the work so it is always possible to anticipate what is going to happen, and investigating possible focal points of problems. When problems are encountered, they must be discussed to the fullest extent that common sense and political judgment allow. Once more, it is clear that the practical experience of the professionals assigned to the project is key to the success of the process. Such experience can smooth the path toward the objectives set by the company.

In order to reach the third objective of the meeting—maintain the commitment to the project—the image the project managers convey during the presentation of the previous topics will contribute greatly. Moreover, it is important that they describe the next steps, what will be done before the next Executive Committee meeting. Additional benefits that can be gleaned from the work to date should be previewed; everyone should be reminded of the importance of maintaining the dedication of in-house personnel to the programmed activities; and open the meeting up for discussions of any project-related topic. A meeting format like the one described here creates an atmosphere in which no one feels inhibited about airing his or her doubts and concerns about the preliminary results or the project's future.

To guarantee that a lengthy and complex project develops to its conclusion, it is not enough to sell it or to approve it. The project team needs to resell it and reapprove it constantly, by demonstrating that it is evolving in an appropriate manner toward the stage at which benefits will be generated as initially anticipated.

8

Phase 1: Understanding the Problem

Looking at the Company and Its Future

The future isn't what you fear, it's what you dare.

—Carlos Lacerda

As has been mentioned, no two package implementation projects are the same, although they may involve the same software product and technology. Each business group, company, or entity is different, because it is composed of groups of different people who have different business (and personal) objectives.

When data was collected back at the time when the project was still being defined, various points arose that prove helpful for project managers identifying issues deserving special treatment when the project finally commences. These points may pertain to an operational aspect of the company's business that will probably necessitate that the software be adapted; to the number of remote locales at which the software will be processed (burdening the telecommunications process); or to inefficient procedures; or to the need to reorganize a specific company function (which presupposes a discussion of such procedures or business organization before decision makers can define how the package will operate for this function). In summary, there is an enormous list of possibilities that are usually noticed by experienced professionals once they start to evaluate the scenario in which the project is to be developed.

The first chore in a package implementation project is to provide the team responsible for doing the work (the consultants and the company's professionals assigned to the project) with a uniform, sufficiently detailed understanding of the company and its business, and about the activities that will be carried out in the course of the project.

For the team working on the project, talking to someone who is intimately familiar with the company and its organization is fundamental to understanding the scenario of the project. The team needs to learn what each sector does, the particular characteristics of the business, who the key people are in each function, how the current systems operate, where the bottlenecks lie, when peak work activities occur and why, whether there are any tax issues that necessitate more complex procedural steps for handling certain information, whether each client is a separate case or if reasonable standardization of market relationships already exists. Depending on the scope of the software project and the complexity of the company's business activity, a set of software functionalities and business issues must be explored so that the project managers can identify how to maximize the operation of the software selected by the contracting company.

Remember also, as stated in Chapter 6, that as part of this process of understanding the business scenario, those responsible for the project need to understand and adjust the expectations of the company's top management with respect to project results. The assumptions that guide the detailing of the work plan are probably based on these expectations. The work plan will need to be finished by the start of Phase 1.

Once the relevant information is collected and a detailed work plan has been prepared and approved, the project's managers must present it to the project team and key users slated to participate in the effort. Everyone must understand what is going to happen, the methods and techniques to be used in carrying out the activities, the estimated time frames, the process for managing the project, the rules of the game (hierarchy, autonomy, schedules, expenses, and so forth), and the role of each individual in the process.

One effective way of constantly reminding everyone of the original plan is to literally place it on the wall of the room assigned to the project team, as a PERT chart or timetable. That way, it can be updated at day's end, so that everyone can track the progress achieved, or the delays incurred. Clearly seeing how things are going is necessary to efforts to maintain productivity.

We must also consider, as I mentioned in Chapter 6, that the software package is a computational tool and thus requires that the technological infrastructure be available for the system to run—meaning that computer(s), or server(s), an operating system, a network, a database, workstations, and so forth, must be on hand. Once the project begins, there will need to be a processing environment in place that is conducive to appropriate performance for those people who are starting to use the software; otherwise, users will be annoyed by the product's response time.

Some consultants reserve time at the start of the project—about a week or ten days—for preparation. During this period, all the activities already described, and other organizational tasks, are carried out so that the project can begin smoothly.

Current Systems and Processes

Now the team is ready to begin. What will be described from here on does not necessarily follow a rigid sequence. Some tasks can occur in parallel or even in an inverse order to how they are presented here. Project managers will plan activities based on their analysis of the scenario in which the project is to be developed.

Implementing the new software package means substituting certain current systems and processes, and adapting particular procedures and controls in keeping with the new functionalities that will become available.

Therefore it is necessary to analyze how the company's current systems and processes operate. The professionals who conduct this survey must thoroughly understand the package to be implemented so that they can see, as they begin to learn how the company presently operates, what the new processes will look like after the project has been implemented.

Sizing up the present situation is a task that requires a certain amount of caution. Team members should be careful not to criticize or ridicule the way certain things are done just because certain processes seem inefficient or antiquated. It is necessary to understand the reasons that certain functions were done a certain way, to prepare the arguments that support suggestions for making future modifications. To be convinced very early on that the users possess information that it will be impossible for the new system to substitute and that the company needs to find a way for the new system to generate—even at the cost of customization—is imprudent. The objective of analyzing the current situation is to understand, in all its details, the environment into which the package will be installed.

It is a good idea to ask users about their reactions to possible process modifications, in light of the capacity of the new system. This gives the team member a way of anticipating the degree of resistance the project will confront when the time comes to discuss alterations to current processes.

To understand current systems and processes, various survey techniques are valid: interviews, workshops, reading the documentation, navigating the present systems, formal presentations, and so on. For each function that is analyzed (upon which the business of the company depends), team members should try to discern which types of transactions are most frequent, how the function in question is related to the rest of the company, and what information is critical to carrying out this function.

All survey results should be documented—with flowcharts, notes, illustrations, examples of forms and documents, or by any other means—so that it becomes possible for team members to put their hands on such material when specific questions arise in subsequent discussions.

Training Key Users

In Chapter 5 we looked at the characteristics and role of the company's key users—the people who will actually have to approve the new work environment provided by the software package. They need to give their input in detail about how the software should provide for each functionality they deem necessary.

To be able to contribute to the project satisfactorily, key users must understand how the package works, as well as the basic concepts that underlie the functionalities the package offers. This objective can be achieved if the company provides comprehensive and detailed training on the software for key users. Generally, such training is conducted by the package vendor, which administers standardized materials developed for the course curricula. The training should be attended by the consultants and by other members of the project team as well. The presence of implementation team members at the vendor training is vital for two main reasons: (1) to guarantee that the training adequately covers the functional issues that have the greatest impact on current processes; and (2) to observe the reactions of key users to controversial (or very innovative) questions in order to detect as soon as possible where the principal project difficulties may lie.

For an integrated software package of a certain degree of complexity, training time is measured in weeks. Requiring key users to attend this training serves as a firsthand example of the dedication to the project that the company expects from its personnel.

Some consultants require that initial training be planned and conducted *before* the project effectively gets underway because they feel that it is impossible to achieve appropriate productivity while the company's personnel still lack a reasonable understanding of the new system.

The question of when the initial training should take place merits careful consideration by project managers. Each case is unique, and a better or a worse approach is not the question here, but rather, what is the most appropriate approach for a particular company. To require the training of key users as a basic condition for beginning development of the work is a way of pressuring the company to transform its declaration of project commitment into reality. It forces everyone in the company to realize, early in the game, that dedication is not just rhetoric but is, in fact, a technical necessity for project success.

In What Ways Is the Company Different from Other Companies?

Tell the truth and run.

—Yugoslavian proverb

By now, the impression that any software package could meet all the apparent unique and specific needs of the contracting company should be disspelled. A more flexible and realistic attitude should have started to take hold, permitting the company to focus on those few and important aspects of the company's business that differentiate it from the rest of the market and to earmark those functions for special consideration and the best solutions. With a mixture of changes in processes and customization of the software, the company will be able to preserve the structure of the acquired system and, subsequently, to improve on the way things are presently done.

As we have seen, during Phase 1 of the software project, the company's unique specifications must be understood in detail, through interviews, workshops, and document analysis. This creates a solid basis for developing better solutions, to be designed during the next project phase (Chapter 9).

In evaluating what is truly unique and specific to the company, it is important to maintain an open mind. Some issues that are viewed as absolutely critical in terms of being fundamental to the form in which the company currently operates may be the result of outdated thinking or assumptions that are no longer valid. These ways of doing things only remain because people cannot break away from the paradigm that originated them. In other words, the reason that an issue is judged to be critical by certain people may exist in their heads, and may not be a reflection of the practical demands of the market. Sometimes outmoded processes can even represent a competitive disadvantage to the company, although people within the company are not yet aware of it.

This is a most delicate matter for consultants, because they worry that their suggestions might be taken as criticism of the competence and intelligence of the company's personnel. Moreover, it is clearly the company's professionals who must feel comfortable with the way the company does business—not the consultants, who are just around temporarily, and who experience the reality of the business only to a limited extent.

For this reason, it is common to witness consultants choosing not to get involved in critical and controversial issues in software projects. It is safer for consultants to try to tailor the system to the desires of the client than to open themselves up to a vote of no-confidence and intolerance, with respect to the project work that is already underway. At times such an attitude results in inadequate solutions (for instance, a customization that alters the structure of the product), and it may even lead to unnecessary additional costs (time and resources spent to develop something that should not even exist).

In recent years companies contracting with consulting services have increasingly demanded that consultants get off the fence and venture their opinions on critical issues. The image of the consultant who in order to tell you the time had to ask to borrow his client's watch is becoming a thing of the past.

Planning for the Conversion of the Initial Data

For those who have yet to participate in package implementation projects, it may sound strange to be concerned about initial data early in the process. After all the company is still months from the time when the data will start to be used. Nevertheless, later in the project this aspect of the project is frequently one of the bottlenecks faced by the software package implementation team. To avert such bottlenecks requires preventative measures, put into place with a careful planning process starting right at the beginning of Phase 1 of the project.

While still in Phase 1 of the project, it is fundamental to map out how the static and dynamic system data are to be made available in the package environment. Static data is data that changes but little, such as information in tables and master files (for example, the supplier master file or a table of all the states of the union), which already exists in a certain current system, or is common to various systems and spreadsheets used by the company. Dynamic data is data that appears when the system is in production (for example, accounting transactions) but may have originated in other systems that interface with the package that is to be implemented.

Professionals who have experience with the software package know the minimum data required for the system to run at the contracting company's facilities. The minimum data includes the short list of files and tables—needed for testing, training, and production—that must be filled out so the system will run. Thus they must identify where these data are located within the company and how to transfer the data to the new system. In implementing more complex software packages, it is common to run across a situation in which some of the minimum data does not yet exist within the company (at least formally). In this event, such information must be prepared by the users and then transferred to the new system (generally by manual keyboard entry).

In practice, the result of all of this work is a list of measures for dealing with how to prepare the data. Typically the list includes the following items:

- programs to be used to convert initial data, that is, programs that read information in the current systems, reformat it to create data that can be understood by the new software package, and then record the reformatted data in the new software programs;

- programs that help users create and key in new data, data that, as yet, does not exist in their systems, but nevertheless is required by the package being implemented;

- data cleansing—many companies take the data conversion preparation as an opportunity to remove obsolete, duplicate, and invalid data, a task that usually requires manual eyeballing; and

- programs that allow the integration of certain current systems that are responsible for generating information to be processed by the software package (through the use of interfaces).

In Phases 2 and 3 of the project, this list of measures will orient the preparation and testing of data conversion and interface programs, as we shall see later.

A realistic evaluation of the effort needed to develop the programs identified in this list is fundamental to adequately assess how resources must be assigned and deadlines determined for preparing such programs. In this manner the necessary programs can be ready when required by the work plan, and holdups with these programs will not jeopardize the estimated start date for pilot testing.

Phase 2: Defining the Solutions

Evaluating Whether the Company Should Go Forward

During Phase 1 the project team's efforts first concentrated on understanding the characteristics of the company's business and deducing which functional or managerial aspects would require a specific solution, or special attention, so that the chosen package could reasonably address all the business's particulars. Also the company was concerned with making the project team and the key users knowledgeable of the software, to the point that they could participate actively in discussions about getting the company's future system up and running.

Phase 1 of the software package implementation project deals primarily with personalizing the problem. In other words, the company attempts to transform a general approach, or methodology, for implementing packages into a specific work plan for making processing feasible for a *specific* package in a *specific* company.

If at the end of Phase 1 (which is called by different names and has a greater or lesser scope, depending on the consultants involved) some of the people at the company feel that the project continues to be generic, that is, the project does not seem to reflect the needs of the company; instead it looks like a job in which the contracting company is only minimally involved. If this is the reaction of the company's decision makers, prudence calls for heeding the warning light. It is time to question and verify whether the team responsible for the implementation really has a grip on the process.

105

If such doubt arises, most probably the consulting team assigned to the project is not sufficiently familiar with the package and is still in the midst of negotiating the learning curve. Another possibility is that the time dedicated to understanding the problem (Phase 1) was insufficient because the time allotted really was quite short or because the consultants assigned to the project lack adequate experience to draw the necessary conclusions.

At any rate, if doubts arise after Phase 1, decision makers need to stop and rethink things. The risks associated with continuing to develop the project without adequate experience and knowledge are very high. Delays, reworking, underutilization of the chosen package, user frustration, and even package rejection become distinct possibilities. At this juncture the positive attitude that has been mentioned throughout previous chapters should dictate that a thorough discussion be called to brainstorm about how to guarantee the project's success. The result of this further evaluation might be exchanging less experienced professionals with people who are more capable of dealing with the situation, replacing the chosen consulting firm with a better one, renegotiating the time frame so the team can complete its learning curve, or repeating Phase 1. All are valid solutions to preserve the project and maintain the objective of implementing the new system.

Rare are cases in which the client company assumes the role of critical evaluator right from the start of the contract. Normally the critical spirit arises only with the arrival of the first problems, and it is often accompanied by a reaction of indignation and surprise at the fact that problems are occurring, after the company has taken such great care when contracting with the package vendor and consultants. As I mentioned previously, the company is the owner of the project, and nothing can ever take the place of the eyes of the owner.

Simulating and Prototyping: Understanding
How the Package Is Going to Work

In Phase 2 it is time to start to transform ideas and theory into practice and results; it is time to plan in detail how the package is going to work for the company. At this stage—normally called simulation or prototyping—the project team will use data and actual company procedures (by this time, well known to the team), gather together the key users, and literally try to run the software to produce the desired results. Obstacles will arise at each step: there will be inadequate procedures, the new system will require new ways of dealing with the data (compared to the current systems), information that was expected to be on hand may not yet exist, some aspects of the business may not be addressed by the package, manual labor will be unnecessarily used—in summary, there will be a series of inconsistencies, all requiring analysis and the discovery of the best solution devised by those involved. Inevitably the team's conclusions will mean a change in present procedures (preferably), or perhaps the team will identify a need for customizing the product (although this is generally undesirable).

But let's begin at the beginning: How does the company prepare for the simulation process? The first step is to model the company in the package. This means filling out the system's basic tables with certain preselected real data (name of the company, product data, clients, suppliers, data from the chart of accounts, and so forth) and values associated with the system parameters (fiscal period, inventory control standards, client categories, just to cite a few options), so that the company's business is reflected in the software to the best extent possible.

Thus at the end of the modeling process it will be possible to recognize that the package has been prepared to process information associated with the company: The screens, reports, as well as some terms and certain functional conditions will look like the company. In practice, when one is dealing with more comprehensive or complex integrated packages, various parameters and conditions will remain to be defined after this first round of modeling simply because they represent new functionalities that do not yet fit with the company's current processes and systems. An analysis must be developed for each of these parameters for possible future implementation. In cases where the package makes possible the introduction of additional functionalities to the company's processes, the prototyping exercise generates new needs for modeling, which, in turn, are then evaluated in a new round of prototyping. This interaction—modeling and simulation—

which is increasingly being adopted by system implementation professionals throughout the world, is also an instrument that can be used to optimize the package's use by the company, as well as a tool for effectively training in-house personnel involved in the project.

The modeling process reveals the need for having professionals on the project team who really understand the product that is being implemented, and it explains why it would be difficult for the company to try to conduct all this work without specialized help. Without the consultants, a company whose personnel lack detailed knowledge of the package would seem to have no alternative other than to contract with the software's vendor to assist the company with modeling and simulation. But using the vendor at this stage is not always a good option, because the vendor's personnel may not have the practical experience or the functional knowledge necessary to conduct this work appropriately.

So how does the process of simulation or prototyping work? The project team installs the modeled package in a controlled technological environment consisting of a server, network, and workstations located in a room dedicated to the project. They gather key users (and later some additional users invited by the key users) into groups, according to the functionality under examination in each session. The functionality may be of a more departmental nature (for example, inventory control), or (following current trends) of a more process-oriented nature (for example, the supply cycle). The organization of the simulation and prototyping work will depend on the software package selected and the contracted consultant's approach.

Most important, the technological environment provided should allow participating users to watch the system process the data, step by step, whether at individual workstations or through some means of projecting the system's screens for all to see. The idea is to achieve active and ample participation by the company's personnel in order to enhance understanding and to create the most favorable climate possible for the implementation of changes. The need for such change will inevitably start to be discovered and appreciated during software package simulation sessions.

Once the environment is adequately prepared, it is time for the project team to take charge of the show. Armed with relevant examples of the company's business transactions (obtained from Phase 1 surveys), the project team members will demonstrate how the new system will deal with each situation, step by step, pausing to discuss each action. These pauses are necessary so that the team can determine whether the users really understand what has happened and why. The overall purpose of the demonstration is to show that it is possible to deal with the daily activities of the business using the new work tools.

Just a reminder: We have already mentioned the importance of having the users' first experience with the package occur in an environment that is conducive to good performance. It should be clear by now why top performance is vital in promoting acceptance of the new software. Talking about changes is difficult enough. Imagine demonstrating the new software in an environment where the response time is unsatisfactory. What a great motive to reject the new system!

Following are some of the typical challenges encountered in the modeling and simulation process:

- The system deals with the information in a manner that is different from what the users expect.

- A current procedure does not adequately fit into the new information flow.

- The system does not meet a specific company need.

- Current procedures may be eliminated because the software can automate part of the process.

Whenever a difficulty occurs, project team personnel should conduct a discussion to put the difficulty into perspective and help users evaluate solutions that enable them to understand how the company will handle that particular aspect of the system in the future. There are typical messages that are delivered at such meetings:

- The system's approach to processing information is valid; it is just a matter of becoming accustomed to this new approach.

- A new procedure will be designed to substitute for the current one, which no longer adequately fits.

- The system must be adapted to meet specific company needs.

- The information flow (or the organization of a company sector, or sectors) will be reviewed so that processing data are generated at the most appropriate moment (for example, the financial and accounting processing of accounts payable are conducted simultaneously).

- Some current procedures will be eliminated.

For many consultants the modeling and simulation process is one of the most gratifying moments of a software package implementation project. Prototyping and simulation are tasks that allow the consultant to combine creativity, group dynamics techniques, and practical experience. Moreover, this is the perfect opportunity for them to win over the client (the company) by inviting its key users to participate in the process.

If the consultant's work is well conducted at this stage, the consultant is guaranteed to earn many additional points on the company's credibility scale—an advantage no consultant can afford to pass up, realizing the difficulties that will inevitably arise as the project goes from paper to the actual processing environment.

Now that we have explored prototyping, it should be more clear why we insisted in the initial chapters on the question of contracting consultants who are experienced in the software to be implemented. It is impossible to maximize package utilization in the company without being able to discuss and evaluate how the new package will deal with detailed aspects of the business, such as its procedures or its specific data. Also it is clear that knowledge of the functional processes associated with the new system is fundamental. After all, the system was originally designed precisely to help companies achieve their business objectives in a more efficient and effective manner.

The prototyping process can take several weeks, and, depending on the scope and complexity of the package, this time may extend to a few months (two or three). The time is the best spent of the entire project. The project team should not try to economize here, but rather economize on the more mechanical tasks, such as programming, testing, and converting the initial data. Simulating how a new system is going to work, besides being an excellent means of training future users, serves to create a propitious environment for the change process to occur, because the sentiment that change is necessary arises naturally from the users as they experience the work environment provided by the software.

Adapt the Package to the Company or the Company to the Package?

To live *is to adapt.*
—Euclides da Cunha

One aspect of the prototying process is worth examining in detail—customization. I have already mentioned several times the need to avoid resolving the problem of adjusting the package to the company by means of software customization. Generally, customization can cause the following problems:

- It modifies the original product, creating a new specific version for the client company. Once the company has the customized version, it might be difficult to update the system when a new standard version is introduced by the vendor.

- Customization can mean additional costs, sometimes not budgeted, besides affecting the project timetable.

- By accepting customization the project team may be avoiding dealing with inefficiencies in the current process, and as a result the new system may inherit such inefficiencies, (in other words, it could incur unnecessary costs).

- Customization is like a peanut: you can't eat just one. It would be very unusual for a list of package modifications to contain *just* a single customization.

Nonetheless experience demonstrates that most software package implementation projects involve some level of customization because, after all, no two companies are the same, and sooner or later specific differences and needs will appear.

To minimize problems caused by customization work, project administrators must know how to deal with the issue in the first place. First of all, it is essential to maintain a firm attitude that customization, in general, is to be avoided. All possible alternatives that eliminate the need to modify the package, including eliminating the reason that has provoked the need to customize in the first place, should be explored to the maximum. Remember, the software implementation process has only just begun, and when it comes to resolving certain problems there is nothing better than time. I like the idea of conditionally accepting particular customizations, and then renegotiating these modifications with users at a later date, when they better understand the new system and can conceive other possibilities. Often this strategy ends up decreasing the importance of points that at first seemed so critical. It has been my experience when in using this approach that the initial list of modifications is commonly reduced to nearly half its original size, without one line of code having to be written, before the customizations even start being programmed.

My intention is not to abhor customizations; often they are necessary to make the implementation of a package in a company feasible. I only wish to make it very clear to future users of new software packages that customization is one of the more risky matters to deal with in the implementation of a software package. And being risky, it should be analyzed in terms of success factors that are critical to the business, rather than just based on business requirements.

On the other side of the coin, adapting the company to the package may bring interesting results for project success and help the project team to comply with established deadlines. Just as was stated in regard to customization that one's attitude should be to *avoid* it, in the case of changing the company to suit the package the objective should be *to make it viable,* to discover a new form of organizing, to modify the current information flow, to redistribute responsibilities, to adapt procedures and controls, to eliminate tasks that have become obsolete (typically keyboard reentry and reconciliations), or to expand the capabilities of certain professionals. All of these examples are valid measures and should be pursued by project managers to make the package viable, with a minimum of customization.

The reason company personnel should demonstrate flexibility may be found back in the software package selection process. The software package was chosen because it could *best* serve the needs of the company. These needs should represent the company not only as it is, but also as it *intends to be* upon implementing the new technology: a more agile company having lower costs and access to better information. Simply changing systems is not enough to make this happen.

Managing Change

The change process is so important, and normally it faces such resistance, that several techniques and methodologies have been developed to deal specifically with this matter. Consulting teams that implement software packages are no longer limited to informatics technicians and project managers. The team must also count on people who are able to promote the process of change itself. Today the tendency is for informatics professionals to learn how to deal with change processes, and for organizational and administration professionals to develop a sound, basic grasp of technology. But this is another story.

When presenting its approach, a prospective consulting firm should also be questioned regarding how it promotes change. It does little good for a company to acquire the world's best package if its people are not prepared for the changes the software will bring.

Many project managers will schedule sessions totally dedicated to discussing the need for, and the process of, change. The objective of these workshops is to establish a new vision of the future work environment, to develop team spirit through team building, and to open up the minds of the company's professionals to new possibilities. In any event, the support and participation of top management is fundamental to achieving success.

In practice, consultants take advantage of prototyping sessions to apply change management techniques in user groups and, as I mentioned earlier, to try to make such changes arise naturally from within the group.

In summary, company executives involved in the decision to acquire a software package, particularly when the investment involves integrated and comprehensive systems, must consider much more than the product's built-in functionality and technology. They must try to envision what type of company they could become when the entire implementation process has been completed. Moreover, the key idea driving implementing new software should be that it is necessary to modify the business's internal processes.

Defining Package Parameters and Basic Tables

Although when discussing prototying we have inserted into the package a good portion of the basic information required by the company's system, we should take this opportunity to explore what filling in such basic data can represent to the company. As we have mentioned, the order in which the various stages of a package implementation project are presented here is only to make them easy to understand. In reality, many of these tasks occur at the same time so that benefits to the company can be maximized during each project phase. This is the case for parameters and basic tables. The very process of prototyping will influence the structuring of certain data that may have been considered not subject to alterations at the beginning of the project.

To better understand why this restructuring has to happen in this way— and why it is important to keep an open mind when reviewing basic aspects of business processes (for example, product coding)—it is enough to remember that the possibilities of extracting information from the package are tied directly to the quality of the information base maintained by the system.

Since the software package was not conceived specifically with the client company in mind, it could be that the field initially created to identify a product code number possesses intelligence, meaning that the field has better possibilities to thoroughly identify a product when compared to the current coding structure, in addition to simply organizing data by product families or organizing it by release date. But let's say that at a certain time company personnel may have defined the release date as the best way to structure internal company codes. Maintaining the company's good old coding may not be the best idea under the new conditions, because of what would be lost in the way of additional product information. Once again, it is essential that project team members thoroughly understand the software so that they can back up their suggestions for altering practices, such as coding, that are firmly rooted in the company.

To cite just a few more examples, following is a list of some items that are normally modified when a company implements an integrated package:

- cost centers;
- charts of accounts;
- the hierarchical structure of the business (regions, areas, warehouses);
- the basis for cost allocations; and
- production routines.

For those who doubt that this is the right moment to think about breaking traditions (or shifting paradigms), we could ask, Could there be a better time than this?

Defining the Customization Required to Meet the Company's Needs

Well, since there was probably no way to eliminate all need for customization, let's look at this process so that we can gain all the possible benefits related to such a decision. The first thing to understand is that the process of customizing is not just one more task in the implementation project; it is a small (at times large) project in itself. And, as in any project, it requires planning, allocation of resources, and monitoring.

Once the customization list is approved by the Executive Committee, an entire process of definition, design, programming, and customization testing must be planned, internal and external resources will have to be allocated, deadlines will need to be established. The time line for customization must be in harmony with the package implementation project timetable to guarantee that the original objective can be reached within the established time. In reality, we need to ask, What resources must we dedicate to the customization process so that the original project timetable will not be compromised? Sometimes this question has no answer. In various cases, no other alternative exists but to delay the implementation project so that critical modifications can be readied before the project team begins to move to the new system.

For current software packages—integrated, comprehensive, and complex—it is almost impossible to think about customization without involving the product vendor. The role of the vendor can be as simple as exercising quality control over the process (to ensure that any modifications leave the package structure undamaged), all the way to assuming total responsibility for the entire customization process. There will have to be some third-party resources assigned to the project, and this adds yet another level of complexity to project management.

Generally, software vendors are not set up to undertake customization projects for clients. They do employ certain professionals who are qualified to do this work, but the schedules these people are usually required to fill include having to support sales, or having to adapt a new version of the product. This means that the buyer of such services frequently ends up negotiating from an unfavorable position, which translates into paying high fees. Thus, the sooner negotiation for customizing the software occurs, the better. Some companies try to structure the conditions for customization work into the original package acquisition contract.

Once all questions involving the development of package customization are resolved, it is incumbent upon project managers—the in-house coordinator and the consulting team manager—to start administering and following up on the customization with the necessary frequency. From here on, the customization process must become part of the Executive Committee's agenda, and it should become a topic of discussion and concern for all involved.

Once more, it is not my intention to argue against customization, but rather to stress that customization is a project requiring the closest of attention by those responsible for the software package implementation process.

Additionally there are specialized customization companies that handle specific software packages. These firms concentrate on dominating the technological environment in which the package runs (databases, programming language) and focus on expanding on the system environment provided by the software package through customization, or they might develop new systems with architectures similar to that of the acquired package. These architectures are designed to be totally integrated into the environment of the main software systems. Company decision makers should consider this resource when planning the implementation project, especially if a reasonable probability exists that the package will need to be modified, or if the company has identified the need to construct new systems for integrating into the package. One example would be the need for a system to deal specifically with client orders before they are passed along to the sales module.

Most consulting firms have partnership agreements with programming firms, or they borrow staff from them. Another route is to make the consultants the package integrators, making them responsible for contracting such specialized labor, as well as for the results produced. That way the company avoids administering yet another service contract, and it can concentrate on monitoring and extracting results from a single source.

Requirements for Altering Existing Procedures

There are times when to be silent is to lie.

—Miguel de Unamuno y Jugo

As previously stated, it is fundamental that the company, represented here by the Executive Committee and key users, maintain a position of total flexibility in relation to the possibilities and necessities of change that the prototyping process may bring to light.

Some changes will be easily discovered and understood during the software simulation workshops, and it is even probable that such changes will be put into action informally before the system begins operation. But the decision to make a change requires special care so that it does not remain only theory. The role of the workshops is to identify the change and deepen the discussion in order to obtain a certain level of understanding and consensus among participating users.

The next step is to do something like what was suggested for customization: develop the change, which involves definition (or confirmation of what has already been defined), design (detailing), formalizing, and testing. In other words, to test a new process, one must literally develop the process to be tested. This means not only changing the work flow, but eventually changing the organization of work, its functions, and its roles.

If the design of the system points to the need for altering more than the sequence of tasks in a particular company sector, formalizing the changes becomes quite important. When a company is installing an integrated software package, it is probable that its present structure and division of responsibilities will be disturbed. Disturbing the structure means modifying aspects such as the distribution of power and even the importance of certain business functions. When we looked at specific approaches and methodology for dealing with changes, these complex questions were what I had in mind. Things won't change without some uneasiness. Remember, playing along with political problems instead of making the organizational changes that are demonstrably necessary will mean underutilizing the acquired package and hampering the productivity that could have been achieved in a more favorable situation.

When it comes to big changes, as we have already seen, consultants differ in their willingness to get involved. There are those who, when faced with the first sign of resistance, capitulate and change the subject, believing that dealing with such a controversial topic is too risky. Others fear for the project's success if these changes are not implemented, so they fight for their ideas. If the company's decision makers are given all the facts and are made totally aware of the consequences, they can make the decision they deem most appropriate.

In practice there are various subjective aspects to decisions about making sweeping changes. To be certain of the outcome, it is necessary to make the change, but if the company is not certain it will be happy with the outcome, should it go ahead and make the change? This is the paradox: to change or not to change? The track records of recognizably successful companies demonstrate one common point: Every one of these companies, over time, has changed at one time or another. They changed products and technologies, trying the most diverse techniques and organizations. They centralized decision making then decentralized it (and vice versa). Not everything worked, but the attempts to change, independently of the results obtained, ended up bringing new perspectives to the business. Talent hidden in the organizational chart appeared and had its opportunity to shine, mistakes brought insight, and unquestionable assumptions were brought down to earth.

In my opinion, if there is an appropriate technical basis for supporting a proposition, it is worth making the change. But the company that intends to change must be prepared for unforeseen adjustments in course, and, above all, its leaders should know how to examine and appreciate what change has brought for the better.

Identifying Interfaces

Today *best practices* dictate considering information systems that support processes and business management not as systems, but rather as a *single integrated system* with the comprehensive functionality to serve the entire company. This single environment is considered ideal because, for instance, the reconciliation of numbers can be totally eliminated. User learning requirements as well as technical support services for the data processing environment can be unified and standardized. The one environment can best reflect the purpose of all business structures, namely to function harmoniously in an integrated fashion to serve clients better. Therefore, the single integrated system constitutes a basic tool for companies seeking to restructure their processes for optimal efficiency and effectiveness, in order to expand and serve their market. In reality, although software research and development work has advanced significantly in recent years, and it is already possible to implement a good number of business functions with single package support, this single environment has yet to become a reality.

Relational database vendors try to demonstrate that their products are the solution to this need because their products allow for "complementing" a basic software package with additional applications, developed "in the same environment." The result: a final set of systems that work as a single integrated system. As previously mentioned, most modern software packages use relational databases as tools to structure their data, that is, the information maintained by the package.

Experience demonstrates that the number of companies already taking advantage of a single system environment is minimal. Although every business manager should be seeking out such an environment, most of us still need to learn how to deal with the question of interfaces in order to adequately implement a software package. An interface is a program, or programs, that permit communication—that is, the exchange of information—between two different systems. These systems may or may not have similar technology. They may even be in totally incompatible technological environments requiring complex interface solutions.

During Phase 1 we identified those systems that needed interfacing with the package for one or both of the following reasons:

- the package needs information generated by these systems; and/or,
- these systems need information to be generated by the package.

Now, in Phase 2, the objective is to design in detail how the interfaces will work, which involves specifying the data to be exchanged between systems; the format in which this data must be recorded so that the system receiving the data understands it; the frequency of interface activation; and the controls required to guarantee that incorrect data is not allowed into the system, or that the same information cannot be transmitted more than once. After these issues are analyzed, the project team should prepare a list of programs to be developed and probably also a list of common business procedures that will be affected once the interface is operational.

The issue of changes in procedures can be understood as an extension of the change process that was discussed in the previous section, but the problem of the interfaces is a little more complex.

Interfaces always have two sides, that of the sending system and that of the receiving system. To develop a program that extracts or receives data from another system, one needs to understand the system, or to obtain support from someone who does. Thus if one of the systems is developed in-house, someone from the company's informatics sector should be assigned to work on the interface program. On the package side, the vendor probably needs to be called in to perform the interface work (as with customization). Moreover, it could be that one of the systems to be interfaced is a package that was implemented some time ago, and its respective vendor will have to participate in the process as well. So it is necessary to plan and assign (and eventually negotiate) the most appropriate professionals to develop the interfaces. Moreover, the task must be fit into the project timetable, so that package start-up is not delayed because the interfaces are not available.

Some software package implementation projects have suffered considerable delays—and can be labeled as failures—because the implementation team did not adequately address the interface process, underestimating its complexity and importance.

Levels of Access, Security, and Control

You have probably noticed that Phase 2 is the heart of the project. In Phase 1 the project team charts the area in which the package will operate and identifies all the relevant points to be treated in the project. In Phase 2 they map out in detail everything needed to be done for the new system to start working in the company. Probably even some conclusions reached in Phase 1 will be subsequently revised by the project team in Phase 2, after more detailed analysis.

To complete this comprehensive work, which is decisive for the success of the project, we still need to consider a topic that, at times, is forgotten for a time during system implementations, but it is no less important than the other topics discussed up to now. We refer to the security of the new system. It should be remembered that the more integrated the system is, and the more its processing is placed directly in the hands of users, the more the question of security must be considered so that an excellent system cannot be ruined because the environment is not reliable or not controlled appropriately.

To start, we probably already know that each data processing environment (independent of the system processed in that environment) and each software program already affords some degree of security and control. Furthermore, systems administrators can assign the system parameters to protect the data. Examples of parameters are individual passwords that limit what the user may do on the system (for example, the password may permit the system to be consulted but not updated); automatic controls that impede an entry from being made for a day or a month in a period that has already been closed; controls that require management approval for transactions that exceed a certain amount; programs for closing out a financial period that verify whether all defined requirements have been fulfilled before liberating the program to perform the operation; and various other possibilities.

Security is also a question of value. The more the company concerns itself with or values security and control, the more such considerations can guide even the choice of the package itself. Yet only a few companies and consultants spend much time on this aspect of selecting the appropriate package, not because of negligence, but because a lot of professionals believe that system security should be dealt with later, once they better understand how the package operates in the company and, thus, once security needs become clearer.

The tendency in companies is to decrease hierarchical levels, to strive for quality at the source (that is, to do things right the first time), and to increase the decision-making powers of managers and employees. Moreover, the idea of a person who owns the information is disappearing. Power is gradually migrating toward those who know how to use the information, leaving behind the practice of using people simply as information keepers. Integrated systems are one market response to this tendency, because they "democratize" information. The current tendency is to loosen up on controls (in comparison to older approaches) as a means of fostering increased agility and decreasing costs. Let us be very clear: the manager whose only job it is to approve something that has already been made does not add value to the final product sent to the client—he or she adds cost.

As we have already mentioned, when new business processes are designed, part of the revision process involves analyzing how to ensure adequate control and a comfortable security level for each function in the new system's environment. Once more, we see how Phase 2 work is interactive and interdependent. An environment that is unreliable or badly controlled can damage a good system. By the same token, an environment that is excessively controlled can stymie a good system and limit benefits to be gained through its implementation.

Interestingly, some (as yet just a few) software package vendors are investing to build into their products the concept of *work flow*. The idea is to supply the system with all the necessary measures to completely and correctly execute a process, permitting the system to know what needs to be done and by whom, after each user interaction. The system then advises the next user that such information is available and what specific steps need to be taken to lend continuity to the work. This mode of operation, besides promoting agility in the carrying out of business functions, also constitutes yet another component to be considered when a company is designing security requirements, because such a system already has some built-in intelligence to decrease the risk of mistakes in data handling.

Once all aspects concerning levels of access have been analyzed, and security and control have been considered, it is up to the project team to define how to implement these needs in the package. It is to be hoped that the security definitions will be adapted to the security characteristics that already exist in the package (and the company's technological environment). The need for some customization might eventually arise from this analysis. In such a case, once again, the package vendor should be called in to discuss possible solutions. Depending on the complexity and the costs involved, the company might find itself in the position of ceding a little, in terms of the rigors of security (in exchange for a certain procedure that takes the place of automatic control), so that the development of the project is not impeded, leaving for a later date further discussion of this pending matter.

Now we only need to deal with the other side of the security question—the physical integrity of the package data and programs. Part of the software implementation process involves designing and implementing operational backup procedures (to provide security copies) and planning for system recovery in the event of failures or information loss. These procedures are defined according to the business's natural processing cycles—daily, weekly, monthly, and so forth—as they are reflected in the software package. In each cycle data maintained by the software is transformed for some purpose, and system administrators need to have the means to back out and reprocess transactions, with a minimum of duplicated work, as well as total assurance that the information so obtained will be consistent.

It is important to make clear that, in order to define backup and recovery procedures that really work when they need to be called upon, two things must be present: First, the project team must be aware of the importance of this issue, have the technical know-how to do the job, and dedicate sufficient time to prepare the necessary procedures. Second, the company's personnel who will be responsible for operating the future system (the informatics personnel and users) must not look upon these procedures as "exaggerated" or go around saying, "Today it's already getting late. First thing tomorrow we'll do it." But then tomorrow comes and goes, and no time is made for backing up the system. When the system crashes and important information is lost, the problem should not be attributed to bad luck. Such a lackadaisical attitude is not acceptable.

Security is a technical issue, but it is also a cultural one. There is no way to generate a totally reliable system environment if people cannot visualize the risks and consequences associated with potential problems occuring with the processing environment, and if they cannot consciously assume a position consistent with these risks, without going around thinking that they are behaving like paranoids.

10

Phase 3: Putting Hands to the Task

Pumping Up the Adrenaline

Success before work only exists in one place . . . the dictionary.
—Albert Einstein

Let's determine exactly where we are in the project. If Phase 1 involved personalizing the problem, as I explained at the start of Chapter 9, Phase 2 is characterized by planning and detailing everything that must be carried out for the software package to be successfully implemented in the company. Therefore Phase 3 is reserved for the largest emotions—now everything that was thought out is to be put into practice. This will require a lot of effort, perseverance, and, principally, the capacity to react to surprises, obstacles, technical difficulties, and the volume of work that lies ahead—especially for the project team.

When a definition is discovered to be incorrect in Phase 3, and reevaluation is deemed necessary, costs are several times (in time and money) what they would have been if the problem had been discovered in previous phases. As we have already seen, in Phase 3 new additions—people and resources—come onboard, including the package vendor, company analysts and programmers, firms or specialized consultants hired to work on certain specific technical matters, as well as future users, subcontracted programmers, and so forth. The work is more or less like those circus acts where the performer tries to keep several plates spinning at once. He has to run from one side to the other constantly to increase the spin of plates that have started to lose speed. The project's managers start to face more administrative work and must divide their scarce time among more people needing help, and the need to make more decisions more quickly.

If Phase 2 is the most important in terms of the *quality* of implementation—because this is where the definitions are formulated—then Phase 3 determines the total time and cost of the project. The total time and cost are, in turn, dependent on the decisions made during Phase 2. In Phase 3 the true experience of the consultants becomes evident—they are seen without their makeup. Also the capacity of the company's personnel to absorb the new work scheme can be evaluated correctly, and without rhetoric.

I like to say that a consultant who has never been involved in a real implementation project, that is, one who has never gone through the process of transforming a plan, an idea, into something practical that works, has yet to complete his or her education as a provider of consulting services. Only those who know the reality of putting hands to the task can plan well what must be done and deal appropriately with the ever-evolving questions that crop up in projects where companies are seeking ambitious changes and goals.

Customization, Interfaces, and Conversion Programs

These three tasks, which were covered extensively in the previous chapter, require enormous attention from project managers, mainly because they involve complex and detailed technical matters, many times beyond the personal knowledge of these people. They must muster all their experience and common sense to evaluate the progress status of data conversion and interface program development or any necessary alterations to the programs.

To start, let's recall that what was said about customization is also valid for interfaces and conversion programs: "The first thing to understand is that the process of customizing is not just one more task in the implementation project; it is a small (at times large) project in itself. And, as in any project, it requires planning, allocation of resources, and monitoring."

It is fundamental that the project's managers consider the need to develop these programs as a project. It is easier to deal with the programs as projects when such programming is subcontracted, because then the program managers can assume the role of buyers of the service. But things are not so simple when consulting personnel working in-house on the implementation, or informatics personnel from within the company, are assigned the work. In this case, things tend to get mixed up.

Generally, the programming will work out if members of the programming team are dedicated full-time to program development tasks, and if they apply an appropriate methodology involving definition, development, testing, and documentation. But such work requires that project managers monitor the project frequently and establish critical points for approving aspects of the programming work—they will eventually need to call in some users to give their opinions as well—so that they can have a handle on the quality and applicability of what is being done.

These programs need special attention because it is quite easy to underestimate the complexity of the problems that can arise—problems with software performance after the introduction of the customization, technical difficulties in extracting data in an environment that is incompatible with the one being installed, or an algorithmic definition destined to generate expected basic information in the new system from an old file but that is not structured according to the design of the acquired package.

Informatics professionals are, by definition, optimists when it comes to their capacity to believe that there are technical solutions for any type of obstacle that appears. Normally, they are easily able to convince laypersons, who depend on such solutions, that everything is under control. After all, laypersons are usually unable to understand the explanation, and they believe that they are in the presence of an expert, or they may feel intimidated about appearing negative in the face of so much optimism on the part of those who must resolve the problem.

If this situation of advance-retreat is not appropriately managed, what will happen at a certain point, without warning, is that users will tire of promises that are systematically unfulfilled, and they will lose faith in the process. They will begin to place unbearable pressure on the project managers, threatening to suspend everything, questioning whether the package really can work for the company, doing anything else to create a pessimistic work climate, and as a result the project team may end up making hasty decisions that prejudice everyone involved.

To avoid this situation, those involved in the project need to know how to develop the programming process; discuss in detail with those responsible for programming how they intend to conduct their job; evaluate deadline commitments, considering contingencies; and, above all, promise users the simple and the feasible, leaving that "something more" as an additional benefit, to be mentioned when it has become a reality.

It is also important to create a separate and controllable test environment for working on customizations, data conversion, and interfaces, one that gives people involved in the project the opportunity to evaluate the quality of what has been developed, without involving other general users in the process. This type of testing, at times called the acid test, is a formidable means of keeping the general users free from unnecessary concerns; it allows those responsible to seek emergency solutions to problems without being under unbearable pressure from outside.

Please, do not imagine we are suggesting hiding problems from users, or from the company as a whole. This tack never works because sooner or later, the truth will come out. I only emphasize that to keep the project under control, project managers and other key members of the project team must be able to evaluate any problem with some degree of privacy, so that the team can determine the best solution dispassionately. Once the problem has been thoroughly analyzed, the matter should be brought before those affected, and/or brought up at the next Executive Committee meeting.

Although customizations, interfaces, and conversion programs represent a critical aspect of the project, there is no reason to believe that the project team will always encounter serious problems with these tasks. If the project's managers understand the importance of the work, use the most appropriate resources, establish realistic deadlines, and, above all, are not remiss in managing the process to develop these programs, it is very probable that all will go well.

Nevertheless, one truth cannot be forgotten: Customizations, interfaces, and conversion programs reflect particular processes and procedures that are unique to the company. The project team should ensure that all materials related to these programs are preserved by the company, because no one else involved in the project will have any commercial interest in saving this material for future use, unless so required by contract.

It goes without saying that the need for keeping documentation up-to-date and complete holds for all project tasks, but we reserve special emphasis for pointing out the need to document programs and their alterations. The contracted consultants and company personnel assigned to the project need to be given the responsibility of documenting in the best way possible each of the programs, or program alterations, developed for the package installation. This includes not only program definitions, or alterations and associated coding, but also an account of the reasons the team decided on each program or alteration, interview notes that detail the problem, and any other document or information that would help reconstruct the rationale for developing a specific functionality. This documentation will help ensure that company personnel in the future will be able to realistically evaluate any new versions of the software and see their impact on the company's installation, because they have the basis for understanding in detail how the interface between the two systems should function, what calculations were made to establish the values for a particular information field, and so forth and so on. Negligence in this matter usually becomes apparent when the analyst who "kept everything in his head" quits, taking with him the knowledge of how to maintain the system.

Implementing New Procedures and Controls

Less risky than developing new programs, but not less complex, is developing new procedures and controls, as mentioned in Chapter 9, where we examined the concept of change and the need for an awareness by key users and top management of the importance of altering the way things are done and, eventually, by whom they are done.

Developing new procedures and controls is a task that is conceptually quite similar to developing new programs. But once the new procedure or control is defined and detailed, programming it means taking several steps to make it ready for practical implementation. Here are the necessary steps:

- Outline the definition developed in Phase 2, generating temporary documentation and a first look at how the procedure or control is to work.

- Discuss the operation with the key people associated with the procedure or control.

- Make adjustments based on what is revealed during these discussions.

- Prepare definitive documentation.

- Formally approve the procedure or control with company decision makers.

In practice, it is not enough to repeat this sequence for every procedure and control. Some procedures and controls have a certain degree of interdependence, and the final solution may involve an analysis of sets of procedures, or even rethinking the structure of the department or function that will absorb the new work routine.

One of the reasons a company acquires a software package of this nature is most likely that the product offers the possibility of simplifying the company's personnel structure. With comprehensive and integrated software, implementing such change is inevitable and will occupy a large portion of project time.

Preparing the Processing Environment

Preparing the processing environment is an aspect of the project that often gets lower priority, and as a result the processing environment can easily become a stumbling block to the work starting in Phase 3.

We have already learned of the importance of starting the project with a part of the definitive processing environment installed, not only to allow users and the project team to experience the authentic situation in which the package is to be run, but also to ensure adequate system performance during training, prototyping, and testing the system, so that users do not become disappointed with product performance and start to question the solution.

Upon arriving at Phase 3, preparing the definitive environment becomes a requirement for the final project tasks to be conducted in the smoothest manner possible. Testing the new system (about which I will speak further later in this chapter), training of end users and converting initial data demand that the processing environment be running practically at total capacity.

Since, in many projects, the consulting team and company personnel are not masters of the technical questions related to the preparation of the processing environment (network installation, remote links, memory capacity, disk space, and so forth), this responsibility is usually delegated (or abandoned) to a few company technicians, or to subcontractors, who often do not sufficiently interact with the project team so that their activities mesh with the established project deadlines and performance requirements.

It is necessary to have a specialized technical group deal with the issue of the processing environment, but because of the very composition of this group (in general, highly technical people) and because of the esoteric character of their talents, it is vital to find a way of organizing the process so as to guarantee that the development of tasks associated with defining and establishing the processing environment are conducted with the same level of quality as has been established for all other planned work.

The package vendor is an excellent information source to help define the required processing resources. The vendor, you will recall, has already been asked to give a recommendation in this regard, back when the company was selecting the package, and the vendor was also heard from on this same subject during project planning. As the company goes through the confirmation process on the technological infrastructure that will support the new software, much additional data regarding volumes, distribution of information, and peak days will become well identified. This makes it much easier for the package vendor to advise the company on defining the company's true processing needs.

Remember, preparing the processing environment depends on the time needed to receive the hardware and other components for installation. At certain periods, equipment can take 90 to 120 days to deliver. This lead time must be considered in planning the preparation of the environment, and it must be factored into the general project timetable.

Another important consideration is that, once installed, a new processing environment will need to be adjusted. Each installation requires fine-tuning certain specific parameters of the operating system, database, and other components to provide the best possible performance under specific conditions. This means that the environment will need to remain under observation for a few weeks or months, undergoing continual improvements until the technicians and users are satisfied with the results. During this adjustment period the advice of a few specialists may become necessary.

What we stated before remains valid: The earlier the project team starts the work associated with technical questions—having to do with the processing environment, programming, and security—the better.

Keeping the Project on Track

Here is some critical advice: Administer the project to maintain it on course, never lose sight of the objectives, and comply with deadlines and cost estimates.

We have already spoken about these points, but we return to them here, in Phase 3, because project management becomes more critical at this time. Problems that arise in this phase lead to delays that can be measured in weeks or months, not to mention hard feelings, disillusionment, and aggressive reactions.

The task of managing the project is one to which the consulting service's project manager and the in-house project manager must dedicate sufficient time to produce, analyze, and define the activities that will steer the project along the best possible course, given the circumstances. Keeping the project on track means constantly checking on the progress of the work and taking preventative measures before the slightest symptom of a problem can occur. But exactly what will these managers be doing?

First they will be looking to see if the time being spent on the tasks in progress is in line with the hours estimated to complete those tasks. There may be various causes for a delay: the initial time estimate was bad; the people assigned to the task were not fully capable of taking on the responsibility; the approach, technique, methodology, or tool adopted for a specific task was not ideal; or there were still points of definition pending, definitions that were prerequisites to completely carrying out the task.

Next, by reverse engineering, they will ask themselves, If an intermediary product of the project must become available at a certain future date, when must the tasks be completed that precede it, and which tasks are prerequisites for the generation of these tasks? If this exercise reveals that the timetable, as originally conceived, will not work, then it is necessary to take corrective measures to clear up the problem. The team managers might, for example, reassign resources to give priority to the tasks in question, thus speeding up their execution. Or they might maintain the resources already allocated and, instead, negotiate for extra efforts, through additional hours or days of work, thus making possible the timely completion of the tasks. Or they might renegotiate the time frame for completing the intermediary product and thereby roll back the eventual end date of the project.

Also, project managers need to remember that "the ideal is the worst enemy of the good," and look constantly to see if, by forgoing temporarily (or forever) a smaller product or lesser objective, the time line and reasonable costs can be saved for the really important things. This is one of the most difficult decisions to make, because it involves a great degree of subjectivity, it can provoke conflicts (with those who think themselves harmed by the decision, or put off), and it may cause some users to conclude that they have bought a pig in a poke, since a portion of what was promised is not going to be delivered.

Deciding to decrease the scope of the work in order to complete the project on time requires analysis, technical justification, and the capacity to negotiate. Key company personnel, such as the in-house project manager and certain important users, need to have the opportunity to discuss and evaluate the proposal with the consultants, thereby mustering support for the suggestion and clearing the path to gain approval from top management for such a change. Surprising professionals working side by side with the consultants with news of such a delicate nature almost always leads to a negative reaction, and to loss of control over subsequent events.

It is worth remembering that, above all, project managers must be attuned to what they can realistically expect to get from each team member and each user involved in the project. It does little good to delegate tasks and wait for each person to fulfill his or her duty. People have limitations; they are motivated for different reasons and do not always appreciate the opportunities placed before them. Justifying delays and inferior quality by pointing out the deficiencies of others does not help maintain the image of a good manager. To understand what can or cannot be delegated to someone and to fight to get the most appropriate resources—this moves people and generates confidence.

Finally, there is still an important point to consider. By Phase 3 a lot of time has gone by since the start of the project (weeks, or probably months), and everyone is starting to tire. There will be comments such as, "When are we going to get this wonderful system going?" "Do you think that some day we'll finish?" "If I knew it was going to be so complicated, maybe I wouldn't have started!" These are only a few of the possible reactions motivated by lots of work and results that still seem far away. Project managers have to plan to cope with the ebbs and flows of motivation and enthusiasm.

Showing the users, at the start of the project, the reality of the process does help, but it does not resolve things once and for all. Project managers will need to continually address issues revolving around morale, to renew hopes, not let the flame of motivation flicker out, provide reasons for maintaining drive and dedication. And in doing this, anything and everything is valid: meetings to report project progress and attenuate doubts and anxieties; social events to maintain team spirit and commitment; a small news bulletin that lets the entire company know that things are happening; awards for various accomplishments; visits to other companies that have gone through similar processes; presentations and films that help reinforce the will to achieve the established objectives; and, *always,* demonstrations that top management is committed to the project and is aware of the effort everyone is making to get the job done.

Stressful, isn't it? No, not always. Undoubtedly there will be moments when a project manager will want to disappear and forget all the responsibilities and problems. But the professional with practical experience, leadership capacity, and the ability to maintain focus on the project's objectives will end up enjoying the role of being a manager and will aspire to once again do something sublime—like putting another system into operation!

Testing the Whole System

At a certain juncture, all the effort spent during Phase 3 will start to pay off—within the established timetable, if the allocated resources have been well employed and the management of the work was effective; if the project has had problems, the payoff may not start to show up until well after deadlines have past. But, at last, a point will be reached when the system finally starts to look like it belongs to the company. Customization is ready, the interfaces also, the procedures and controls have been reviewed, the security features are well defined, and the processing environment has been set up (or almost).

It is time to verify whether this entire apparatus works right and is adequately adjusted for use by the dozens, or hundreds, of users who will be interacting with the system when it comes online. Testing the system is an extremely important task, yet it is often conducted hurriedly or only to a limited extent, because, generally, projects suffer delays, and one way to make up part of the lost time is to shorten the testing period. What we have said earlier about how informatics personnel are excessively optimistic people when faced with technical problems also holds for how they approach systems testing. They often start from the principle that having dedicated so much of their work and care to the system, well, all of this just naturally must have generated a product that, although it might still have a few tiny mistakes, it wouldn't have any significant errors that could compromise the project at this late stage in the game.

With this premise in mind, they attempt to quickly satisfy themselves by conducting simple and not particularly comprehensive tests, instead of really trying to break the system so as to avoid being surprised when users at their workstations encounter big problems dealing with the company's vital business data.

For an integrated and comprehensive system, it is practically impossible to anticipate every conceivable situation that should be considered. Therefore those responsible for implementation must realize that unforeseen situations can occur in the future (the future being a month or a year after operation commences). Such situations will cause disruptions to the company and require agile solutions. It follows, then, that the project team should try to minimize such uncertainties by testing in an organized fashion and to the best of their ability anything imaginable, given their present knowledge of the new work environment.

Four points must be taken into account by whoever plans and conducts these tests:

- Users should participate in the tests.
- Procedures and programs should be tested together.
- Tests should also evaluate system performance with realistic volumes of data for processing.
- Tests should be planned according to the natural processing cycles under which the new system will operate.

The participation of users ensures that many of the company's actual business situations will come to mind and can be tested beforehand. Remember, this is a job where all help is welcome, in function of the volume of work involved. Inviting end users to participate is a good means of providing training in the new environment (although there is to be a formal training right after testing).

The idea of testing procedures and programs together is important. The project team is no longer concerned with looking for errors in programs or determining whether routines have been well planned; these are prerequisites for testing systems. What needs to be established at this point is whether the new work environment provided by the new system operates in the best possible manner, throughout its entire functionality and scope—from entering data to managing reports, from handling standard transactions to carrying out credit adjustments or returns, from working through the daily routine to managing the annual closing.

It is important to evaluate the performance of the system under the large volumes of transactions that can be expected in the course of daily business. It does no good to believe that it is fantastic that a particular update took *only five seconds* to execute, only to subsequently discover that twenty thousand such transactions will need to be processed per day, and that at the rate the system is working, operating twenty-four hours a day will not be sufficient to keep the system up-to-date.

In the most modern processing environments—client/server and relational database—the need to adjust performance is still frequent, and this reality cannot be underestimated during the project. Performance is something that must be investigated and tested all the time, because solutions are not always trivial.

For this reason, following the fourth suggestion—plan the tests according to the natural processing cycles—can help improve the system quality and the extent of the benefits to be achieved by the implementation. A processing cycle is a set of activities—manual and automated by the system—executed to complete a business process. Following are several examples of processing cycles:

Daily Cycle

Activities that are repeated daily, such as accounting entries, sales orders, purchases, inventory transactions, payments, cash flow, and so forth.

Weekly Cycle

Sales reports, preliminary closings, statistics, and so on.

Monthly Cycle

Closing out the month, determining sales commissions, budget follow-up, management reports, payroll, and so forth.

Registry Cycle

New suppliers, new clients, credit analysis, and so on.

Other Cycles

Budget revision, determination of performance indicators, and so forth.

All the documentation and experience accumulated during Phases 1 and 2, particularly during the prototyping process, as well as the material developed during Phase 3, will serve as a basis for defining what processing cycles should be used for testing.

For each of the identified cycles, it is necessary to plan a sequence of tests. Members of the project team will write up a plan that indicates what is to be tested and how, the situations to be tested, the associated data that must be provided to the system, and the expected results. The expected results, the values or information that should be generated by the system and procedures, should be calculated beforehand so that they can be compared with the results generated by the test. When there is a discrepancy between the expected results and those obtained, the cause of the difference will need to be analyzed so that the project team can make the respective corrections and retest the functionality until no doubt remains.

If the project managers coordinate the testing stage well and produce documentation that allows verification that everything has been done, the eventual problems arising in Phase 4 (when the system is put into operation) can be easily resolved, and their causes more quickly detected.

Testing is considered a tedious activity by many system implementation professionals. It does become tedious if the testers focus only on the mechanical side of the tests: putting in data, taking out data, and seeing if it works correctly. To avoid falling into the trap of apathy and prejudicing the quality of the results, the testers should see the tests as previews of the new system, presented to an audience of selected guests. After all, those testing the system will be the first to have contact with the new work environment. They will receive a privileged insight into how the company's business will be operated in the near future, and they will be able to savor, early on, what has been accomplished. For company professionals involved in testing, this represents the chance to see where career growth opportunities will lie so that they can direct their efforts as soon as possible in the right direction.

Errors identified during the testing cycles may lead to reevaluation of programs, procedures, definitions, and even project assumptions. It is important to consider that the later in the project a correction is made, the greater its impact will be on the timetable and related costs. The tendency to accommodate the correction in the quickest and cheapest possible manner is widespread and tempting, and it might even be feasible. But project managers should be careful to analyze their options when faced with an error with big consequences and avoid making a precipitous decision. It is worth evaluating whether this is not a case to be brought before the Executive Committee, or perhaps it should be decided with the input of certain key users.

If there are still any doubts about the apparent rigidity suggested here for conducting system tests, here is an additional argument. The testing environment is still a controlled one, that is, one under the well-protected guardianship of the project team, allowing for analysis and correction of errors to take place with a certain privacy. When the final training starts (see the next section), the system goes public. Any problem revealed at this stage generates pressure from all sides, and the project team can be overwhelmed. It is better to have more certainties than doubts, even if it is necessary to work beyond the normal time schedule, than to arrive at the training stage of the project and still have to count on luck and optimism for good results.

Training Future System Operators

The final test has been completed and the project team is now confident that the project will be a success. It is time for everyone to cross their fingers and begin delivering the system to its true owners: the end users. The role of key users, handpicked at the start of the project, becomes greater at this juncture. They will be active during the training and, eventually, will serve as instructors and agents to replicate the skills acquired during the project. But their chief tasks are to demonstrate confidence in the results and to use their credibility with other users to muster all the collaboration and enthusiasm possible. Key users can be a great help in making everything flow well from this point forward.

The first step in transferring the system to the end users is training. Users need to learn how to run the system safely and assimilate the concepts structured into the new work scheme, so that the desired benefits can really be achieved. The training environment should be carefully prepared. The sessions can take place in an environment specially arranged for this purpose (generally, this is the best solution), or they can take place where each group of users works (which assumes that the final environment is already practically ready). There are advantages to the first option, making it more conducive to training. Since business processes have been altered (or will be shortly), it is probable that people from different sectors will need to be assembled during the training. Moreover, current systems will have to continue to run, and the users' work sectors will be congested by all the extra equipment.

The technological environment must provide the best performance possible during training so that unnecessary negative reactions can be avoided. To show that everything is under control, trainers should inform users of any performance problems that still persist at the time, so users don't stumble across the problems themselves.

Real data that is known to the users should be used to facilitate identification with what appears on the system's screens and reports and to promote understanding of how the system works. The project managers should understand that although for them this stage is training, for the end users it is the test stage. They want to learn, but they are also concerned about verifying, for example, that their work will not double under the new system, and, of course, they will look for evidence that the numbers produced by the new system are in fact reliable.

It is useful to plan for training to be organized in the same way as testing, that is, by processing cycle. That way the training experience reproduces the reality that users will confront once the system goes into operation. It also helps participants better define their individual roles in the new processes. These roles will have already been analyzed during the stage when procedures and controls were revised, so training is a way of evaluating the true capacity of certain workers to assume the responsibilities reserved for their positions or functions. Some people end up discovering new opportunities in moments such as this.

The project team should be prepared to provide quick and precise responses to innumerable doubts and criticisms that arise during training. There is nothing that generates more disbelief in users than having their questions badly answered, or being told that an answer depends upon contacting some specific person (whom users might or might not even know) who is the only one capable of clearing up the doubt. So it will be necessary not only to involve professionals in the training who really understand the package, and its implementation characteristics for the company in question, but also to set up an information network that permits quick access to the best sources for answers to various questions that will arise—technical, functional, organizational, fiscal, and managerial.

Some people might ask whether the software package vendor should be called in to conduct this type of user training. The answer is no, the vendor should not take charge of the training program, but the vendor certainly should participate in training matters that are directly linked to its product, or serve as a consultant on the information network.

The training we are addressing here involves the company's specific implementation of the software package, which, at this point, involves other systems (through interface), customization, and procedures and controls that are related to the particular characteristics of the company. The professionals who are best prepared to conduct this training are those who conducted the simulation, design, and management of the customization, data conversion, and interfaces, and who know exactly why each solution was developed.

That is why certain key users are encouraged to assume the role of being training instructors for the end users. These people are among the best prepared to explain—and defend—the new work design. Moreover, they enjoy credibility before their peers.

Just as the training at the start of the project, directed toward learning about the standardized operation of the package, lasted for several weeks, this latter training can also be of several weeks' duration, in function of the scope of the system. Keeping users confined to a training room for several days, away from their normal work activities, is a big challenge, but it must be done. The cost of inadequate training at this late stage will show up in the next phase (Phase 4), when the system is up and running and the actual processing begins. Ill-prepared users will need greater support in order to operate the system, and this translates to more consulting hours allocated to the project and a certain processing clumsiness during the first weeks that could generate doubts about the efficiency of the new solution (requiring much convincing to undo).

It is worth remembering to invite someone from top management to reinforce the project's importance, and to demonstrate why it is vital to support the initiative and make every effort to ensure that things go well. Such words, coming from the top, can help—and how! Presentations that are done well at the start and the conclusion of training sessions for various user groups will testify to the company's commitment to the project, as well as reinforce the fact that there is no turning back: The new system is no longer an idea, it is reality.

11

Phase 4: Making It Happen

The Time Is Drawing Near

Dreams are free. Transforming them into reality has a price.
—Ennis J. Gibbs

The peak activities of the project are close. All the dedication and efforts, the discussions, fears, problems and their solutions, the administration of time and resources, the enthusiasm about advances in the way work is done, intermediate results—all come together in Phase 4. The software package, selected and acquired so long ago, is to become the newest company system, like a sign of new times (fertile and prosperous) that lies on the horizon.

For those who see in projects of this nature more than a professional obligation, this is a moment of poetry and of anxiety. It is like visiting for the first time someplace that you always wanted to go. But this is no time to drop one's guard and relax. In spite of all the precautions, it is still possible for new problems to arise at the last minute, at a stage when the users and the company will have little patience for delays and for mistakes to be corrected. So it is fundamental that the project team be ready to act rapidly and, if possible, take preventative measures. Now, more than ever, the team members need to plan step by step what is to be done, anticipate the results, create contingency measures, reserve extra time to see that everything truly goes well, conduct evaluation meetings to gauge how the work is going, and to encourage people.

In Phase 4, as in all previous phases, there are no miracle prescriptions. There are always alternatives that must be analyzed carefully so that project managers can decide what seems most appropriate for the company. The crucial question is, When is it the right time to abandon the old systems and begin to formally and officially process data using the new software package?

Establishing an Operating Environment

Before we can begin to think about processing data with the new system, we need to look at some components that must be well adjusted so that this change of systems is possible. The project team has been working to construct the future processing environment since the beginning of the project. At this point that environment is no longer in the future; it exists. Pending activities of any nature with regard to the technological environment must be resolved completely, so that nothing gets in the way of processing with the new system. Typically, the following points must be monitored along the way so that the operating environment can be ready and available:

- the acquisition of workstations and their installation in appropriate locations;
- the standardization of workstations (configuration);
- cabling to install network points at the appropriate locations;
- small construction jobs to provide an appropriate work environment;
- the placement of antennas to transmit and receive data (via satellite or radio);
- the communications infrastructure of telephone lines, data transmission lines, and/or fiber-optic lines;
- the acquisition and installation of printers;

- equipment maintenance contracts;
- the formalizing of backup and data recovery procedures; and
- cleaning up any unnecessary databases and eliminating programs that will no longer be used.

Depending on the specific technological environment, other points may arise, or some of those just mentioned will not be applicable. It is not prudent to wait for the project to reach Phase 4 before becoming concerned with the operating environment. Many of these tasks can be taken care of beforehand, and it is wise to preplan this work. The final operating environment represents the evolution of the configuration from the time that the project was first planned, when the package was acquired, up through when it was adjusted after prototyping, customization, interfaces, and testing because some technical limitation or performance problem was indicated.

For the operating environment to be adequately prepared, it is recommended that the team work with a checklist (a list of pending items), one containing lead times, deadlines, the names of people assigned responsibility for each listed task. The company's informatics personnel are normally heavily involved in preparing the operating environment, since they are the ones who will administer the system once the project ends.

It is recommended that the team do something on the order of validating the physical infrastructure prepared for system operation. Usually this can be done by the software vendor, which can assign technical people not involved in the project to develop an independent opinion about infrastructure readiness.

Data Conversion

Another important component in preparing to switch systems is converting the data for use in the new system. This point has already been covered in Chapter 8, where Phase 1 of the project was described. At this point in the project, there should no longer be doubts about how the information will be loaded as initial data in the new system. A portion of this data should already have been loaded, become available, and even updated in previous phases of the project, because several important project tasks—prototyping, testing, and end user training—needed real information in order to be developed more efficiently. At any rate, when it becomes time to change systems, the work must be completed and all available information should once again be verified.

In Phase 4 the package files and tables will be totally filled in with company information, and the software will then assume once and for all the face of the company. Yet for some initial data the decision to load it into the system is a little more complex. In particular we are referring to information that varies with time or that represents the business's history. To be clearer, let's look at some examples of the kind of data we have in mind:

- account balances;
- unpaid client invoices;
- supplier invoices yet to be paid;
- the sales history of a client;
- the purchasing history for raw materials;
- information from previous years to be used for comparative purposes;
- the maintenance history of equipment;
- statistics on the quality of service, and so forth.

Although changing systems signifies more and better functionality for users, it does not always permit converting all the information from the old system into the new, for various reasons. There may be difficulties in reformatting the data to store in the new system, it may be impossible to manipulate certain data in the new system, the new system may treat certain information in a different way, or additional work may be created by transferring certain data, and there may be other technical and functional problems.

Therefore it is necessary to conduct an analysis (which should start in Phase 1) to determine what data is really worth investing time and money to preserve. For example, some historical information might have been important in the past because the old system did not operate in real time. But by using a new software package with more resources, such information may no longer be so relevant.

Changing business processes, about which we learned in examining Phases 2 and 3, may end up modifying the need for information within a certain sector of the company in order for its people to carry out operations. For example, today software packages permit users to calculate the profitability of an order at the start of a sales transaction. Having precise and up-to-date cost information is more important, in this case, than maintaining a record of the previous five years of purchases made by the client in question. The point is, by changing systems and processes, the data critical to the business also changes.

For more dynamic information, such as balances and financial documents coming due, the start date of the new system operation can be a problem. The programs used to load initial data must transfer a set of information to the software with a calendar date that is consistent with that on which the load was made, so that henceforth the new system can update such information. This need to establish a cutoff date for the package, while the outside world continues working without stopping, explains why converting data for use on a new system ends up taking place on weekends, the eves of holidays, or late at night. It is a way of stopping the company (presuming that activity during these hours is limited or nonexistent). In today's times, this cannot always be done for all businesses, and more and more creative solutions and, principally, precise controls on the process of information transfer, are needed.

Finding the Best Approach to Safely Changing Systems

Everybody knows that the old systems are to be turned off at a certain point, and that the new system, represented by the software package and its customization and interfaces, will go permanently into operation, inaugurating a new era for the company.

The problem is that the rest of the world—clients, suppliers, the government—will not stop so that the company can change systems calmly. How, then, to proceed? An expression widely used in today's market, "changing the airplane's turbine in flight," illustrates what company personnel feel when the time comes to make the switch, often called the *conversion*.

Once more, there are no magic rules. But there are various approaches that companies can use to adjust, some better than others, to the circumstances of implementing a new software package. Generally, we can classify these different approaches into a few categories:

- direct conversion;

- parallel conversion;

- pilot conversion;

- limited parallel conversion; and

- retroactive parallel conversion.

Readers are probably aware that the most popular conversion approach is the *parallel approach*. But let's examine each option to come to our own conclusions.

Direct conversion, that is, turning off the old systems on the day the new system goes into operation, presumes a high degree of confidence in the results to be obtained during the first days of operation. This tack involves not only adopting the premise that there will not be mistakes or significant problems in the new system, but also that the performance of the users will be very good and that company operations, legal reports, and other information required for making decisions will be totally correct and immediately available. This is because the business, as I have said, cannot stop.

Before we discard this conversion approach out of hand, classifying it as excessively risky or even unfeasible, let's wait just a second. It is true that there are very few practical cases where direct conversion has been employed, and in some cases it did not work. But the cause of failure does not lie in the approach itself, but rather in the consistency between the manner in which the project was developed and the conversion approach that was chosen.

The choice of conversion type must take into account the actual circumstances of the project: the quality of the people involved, their level of knowledge of the technology used, the level of participation by key users during the project, the complexity of the functionalities implemented, the extent of the tests already conducted and their results, the degree of standardization of company operations, the time of the year in which the conversion will take place, the support of top management, and an evaluation of the degree to which end users have taken advantage of the recent training opportunities. Putting it this way, one can see that a certain possibility exists for choosing a direct conversion.

In reality, direct conversion is an ideal approach, because it speeds up the availability of the new work environment and does not overload personnel with extra duties (such as having to work both systems simultaneously). But software implementation projects do not usually enjoy ideal development conditions owing, principally, to limited resources (financial and human). Therefore project directors may opt for other more secure approaches.

Parallel processing is normally considered a more secure approach. The idea here is literally to process the two systems—the old and the new— simultaneously, comparing the results of both, step by step, in order to confirm that the new system is correct and that users know how to operate it without creating problems.

The difficulty of this approach is the amount of work it entails; under the best of circumstances the workload will double. With this approach it is vital that both systems work in tandem so that comparisons can be made using fresh information, and discrepancies can be studied, understood, and corrected immediately. The old system is still considered the official one, but the data being placed into the new system becomes official as soon as the signal is given to pull the plug on the old system. Therefore, both systems must be operated as official for a period of time and, hence, the larger volume of work.

Another problem with parallel conversion is that the old and new systems are not the same. The new system contains a series of additional functionalities that must be dealt with during parallel operation. Therefore project team members will need to talk with the users who are going to operate both systems for a certain period, seek and obtain their collaboration, and maintain good morale during this process. When there is a change in technology, this means having, for example, mainframe terminals and network workstations coexisting in the same location, contending for space with the users.

The parallel approach presumes that certain significant problems may still occur. Therefore it is necessary to prepare to act should these problems arise. An emergency brigade, composed of consultants, informatics technicians, and key users must be at the ready to minimize the effects of any mistake or inconsistency that arises, so that system processing will not be delayed. Moreover, a serious error at this time can bring the parallel operation to a halt, necessitating a reinitiation of the process once the problem is resolved.

The following three operations—pilot conversion, limited parallel conversion, and retroactive parallel conversion—are variations on the parallel approach. They maintain the idea of processing both systems simultaneously, but they seek to decrease the workload by concentrating the team's efforts on sampling the operations to allow the project team to evaluate the new work environment and select the best moment to disconnect the old system.

The *piloting approach* is based on the idea that parallel processing can involve processing a portion of the total business. So the new system could be run for a certain region, production line, type of operation, factory, or even for only a certain group of people. The processing environment is then adjusted during piloting, and the new system setup is then replicated quickly throughout the remaining parts of the company. Users who participate in the pilot process normally assist the project team to replicate the process elsewhere.

With the *limited parallel approach,* during conversion the project team is not concerned with creating the definitive databases to be used by the new system. The objective is to extend the system test, using a good sample of real data. For example, for each day of operation under the old system, two or even three days will be spent operating the new system. This means that the new system can be operated more tranquilly, without the pressure of a cutoff date. The objective is to verify that the results coincide and that processing has developed well.

The *retroactive parallel approach* causes the least tension in users: with this method all the operations are processed for a certain period of time that is already concluded and for which results are known. This means that while the old system maintains up-to-date information, the new system is processing at a variable rate, depending on how the day-to-day operations of the company develop. At the close of the month, for example, the retroactive parallel approach is suspended for a few days and then returned to, once the workload eases up.

As has been previously stated, none of these approaches in inherently better than the others. Experienced consultants will evaluate the company's culture, the development of the project, the people they are working with, and the stability of the technological environment, and then they will suggest or defend the conversion approach they believe is compatible with the company and the project.

Most important, however, is gaining user support during this final challenge. Although end users will still need help, as will be mentioned later in the chapter, users are the ones who must make the new system happen. They have to understand the conversion approach that has been selected, buy into the idea, be aware of the efforts and responsibilities involved, and feel that the sooner they demonstrate mastery of the new system, the sooner this new, irreversible reality will be installed. At this stage it is to be hoped that users are anxious to work in the new systems environment and consider its irreversibility to be a positive thing.

It is very important to check that users are ready for the change. Was the training sufficient to prepare them for the new functions and operations? Do they understand the new business processes? It is recommended that the company seriously consider another test, this time focused on checking user readiness to operate the new system. Unlike a test for checking or rechecking the software configuration and the performance of the technological infrastructure performance, this test of user readiness should be developed with the real working environment in mind—data, transactions, master files—reflecting real situations. It can be seen as another training—on the job training.

How Long Should the Conversion Take?

In the previous section we covered the different conversion approaches. Each of them, with the exception of direct conversion, involves dedicating a certain amount of the users' time to working with both systems, the old and the new, so that the project managers and the users themselves become confident enough to make the changeover. But just how much time is needed for this to occur? A week, a month, three months? Should the project managers impose a deadline?

It is important to have a concrete goal to strive for. Establishing a certain day on which the company will disconnect the old system forever is a way of creating a challenge and an objective for all. But the date must be realistic given the circumstances of the project and the conversion approach selected, or else when the designated date arrives, another new goal will probably have to be set—this time "for real"—leaving people with a feeling of frustration.

If we were to solicit the opinions of various professionals in the market, consultants and users alike, we would discover that the ideal amount of time needed for a conversion is about one month. One month normally represents a complete cycle and a business measurement unit, and within that time most of the projected operations for the software will have taken place. It is reasonable to imagine that upon concluding a complete cycle successfully, the new system will be capable of supporting the company's operations.

Another reason why one month is commonly settled upon is the presumption that the company will not be willing to pay for more project team time—consulting time, principally—and that decision makers will believe it is time for the users to start walking on their own two legs.

The question of fees leads many consultants, when they initially present proposals for their services, to underestimate the time needed for package conversion. Their fear of making the project price unattractive leads them to cut total projected time, and the result can be the sacrificing of important tasks. Earlier in the process the consultant may reason, "It is not possible for the personnel of this company to need more than one month to totally absorb the new system!" Or "As the company starts to sense the quality of our services and the benefits of our work, it will be much easier to negotiate additional project time. We're doomed if we try to demonstrate right now that this time will be necessary. Besides, I bet the competition will do the same thing!" These suppositions do not always work. If, in fact, it was not possible to estimate before starting the project precisely how much time the conversion will take, this time should be pinned down as soon as it becomes possible to make a reasonable estimate. The later this is done, the worse it will be.

For restricted or stand-alone packages (financial programs or maintenance systems, for example), one month can be established as a goal, although it is always wise to reserve additional time for lighter support (part-time) during the following month (the first month of real operation).

For comprehensive and integrated software, in the final years of the 1990s, the tendency is for the situation to be a little more complicated, especially if various modules are to go into operation all at the same time (or all of the modules at the same time). In this case a longer conversion process, probably using the piloting or the limited parallel approach at the beginning, and a complete parallel approach at the end, may lead the project administrators to plan for a conversion lasting from three to four months, even though such a prolonged process can be very difficult on users. Another possible approach is to conduct a shorter conversion process, say of one month's or two months' duration, but maintaining the project team and consultants to oversee the operation of the new system for some time after that. That way the system can be monitored daily, under circumstances quite similar to those described above for the direct conversion approach.

Perhaps given the explanations so far it is becoming easier to understand what planning a direct conversion involves. The project must be developed in such a manner that everything to be checked and adjusted during a parallel, or a pilot conversion, as well as the eventual preparation of the users who will operate the system, must occur before the conversion period.

On the other hand, other types of conversions do not therefore demand less quality in project management. But the project management process is by necessity a little different for the other conversion approaches, which can be, shall we say, more flexible.

User Support during the First Moments

We have already stressed the importance of keeping the project team on to help users during the first weeks, or months, of software operation. In this period, the company's users are still at the beginning of their learning curve when it comes to knowledge of the new system. Prototyping, training, and tests have undoubtedly helped them to progress a certain way along this curve, but there is nothing that substitutes for practical experience. There is a solid basis for taking maximum advantage of what can be learned by direct contact with the system. The speed at which the level of skill will grow is startling, especially if users feel well supported and are thus unafraid to purposefully try out the available functionalities.

Setting up a help desk group is a practical solution to the need to support new users, especially in the first moments of operation. The help desk should be maintained after the project ends in order to provide continuous support for users in the new working environment. Those who staff the help desk should be able to answer the common questions and know the right person to whom to refer the more complex issues.

The project managers should not underestimate the importance of the initial period of operation, nor should they be unduly impressed early on or overly enthusiastic about seeing the software go into operation. Their attitude should be extremely optimistic when talking with users, but conservative when planning and analyzing follow-up of the initial processing period.

So what types of problems can occur? First, there can be certain program errors that have not been sufficiently tested (or simply tested badly) when the project team attempted to anticipate possible conditions in the real business world of the company. When it comes to finding a solution to a program error, the difficulty of the task is always an unknown. Also, let's recall the eternal optimism of informatics personnel, who think that no problem exists in their programs that cannot be quickly resolved. Faced with an error, it becomes necessary for them to create a bypass solution immediately, perhaps involving some manual procedure or creating a temporary, simpler program to maintain the information in the system. Whatever solution is found, it should be sufficient for users to live with the limitation for a few days (or weeks, as the case may be), without suffering a loss of confidence in the system.

Another obstacle may be a technical problem that interrupts processing, generating messages that indicate errors in the technological environment (whether caused by the system or not). This situation should be addressed by personnel qualified to deal with the situation. The difficulty may arise because the system has exceeded the preestablished memory limits, or because the database presented some type of information inconsistency that is blocking any additional processing, or for various other possible reasons involving equipment or the operating system. Technical errors scare users, because to them it looks as if something very complex and sophisticated is out of control. For such problems, a temporary solution may be to decrease the processing volume, make backups more frequently to minimize recovery time, or even suspend certain functionalities that seem to be responsible for causing the interruption.

There is also what is conventionally termed bad performance. Everything works but very slowly. (More than twenty-four hours are needed to process a complete day's work. This is impractical.) Maybe the reason is that the actual volumes are way beyond what was planned for, or the tests did not make clear that volumes would be a problem. Slow performance is not always simple to remedy. Routines in the user workstation must be transferred to the processing server (which is quicker); program codes must be reviewed with the goal of optimizing equipment usage; maybe real-time updates need to be processed later in batches so that users can avoid regularly having to spend a few seconds, or several minutes, in front of their workstation unable to access the system. When working on a solution, it is fundamental to involve the vendor of the specific component that is affecting performance.

A final problem (although I have not exhausted the possible problems) is on the business processes side. On paper, and in the workshops, the new organization and new form of doing things may seem optimal. But in practice things seem to be somewhat unwieldy. Perhaps, in spite of the training, users have not completely absorbed the new concepts. The cause could also be of another origin: political. The new organization of processes created a redefinition of responsibilities and the hierarchy in place before the change has been affected in some way. Some people, feeling put down or diminished in their status by this fact, or simply not agreeing with the idea of a greater democratization of information, may be creating imaginary obstacles to impede the communication flow among the various sectors involved. Often this is the true reason that things do not go as expected. The causes can be diverse, but the solution is always found in trying to engage in dialogue, in reinforcing concepts that have already been discussed, recalling the vision being pursued, and reminding all of the need for team spirit. An extreme case of lack of collaboration may require a more energetic attitude on the part of top managers so that the project does not lose the support of the majority of users. What is important is that the new system does not stop. To return to depending on the old system at this point can be disastrous to the credibility of the software.

Making Identified Adjustments

Life during conversion is not only filled with problems and emergency situations. If the project has been well planned and well developed, it is probable that the disagreeable situations just discussed will not even become a bother, and the conversion instead will be filled with moments to remember.

As users start working with real data in the system they may discover opportunities for improving the new system and the newly implemented processes. The temptation to go back and fool around with the programs and the organization of the processes is tremendous, given that the benefits seem to await the users, but this temptation should be reined in, and common sense must prevail. It will always be possible to improve a system and the processes associated with it (see the next chapter), but the goals of the software implementation project must be maintained. So each opportunity that arises for making an improvement must, in principle, be considered conservatively. The extent of the benefit, or the justification for making a change, may be insufficient to justify sidetracking the conversion process.

The ideal is to invest some time in understanding the scope of possible improvements—but just enough time to prove their validity and benefits. Once this analysis has been completed, there are two alternatives: either the change is deemed unjustified and should be abandoned, or the change appears interesting but not critical, and it should be added to a list of future improvements to be tackled during the postimplementation period.

If, as I just said, the change is really necessary or critical, it is probably an issue that was not detected during the project work—and it is a problem in need of correction. Such discoveries are always very embarrassing, because the present moment is not one for reworking but, rather, one for making things happen.

Producing a list of improvements for the future is a healthy exercise, and it can demonstrate to users that the system will remain dynamic. In the meantime, it is best to keep in mind that a well-selected and well-implemented software package is one in which improvements will mostly likely evolve from the original functionalities and processes. Additions or substitutions will occur when new versions of the product become available from the vendor (see Chapter 13).

12

Now That The Package Is Working, What Should the Company Worry About?

Is It Possible to Improve the Use of the
Package and Achieve Greater Benefits?

After so many months, the tangible work of the implementation team is there for everyone to see. The new software is an investment that most certainly will bring various planned benefits, and maybe even a few other good surprises. At this juncture, the photographs of the heroes and those responsible for the success have already been taken and published.

Okay, so now are we finished? No, and I can assure readers that while this system is running, there will always be things to do. In the previous chapter we saw a list of future improvements that should be prepared, consisting of possible alterations detected during the conversion process. Also, as described in the discussion of Phase 2 in Chapter 9, some customization should be accepted provisionally for future review (either during the project or in the future).

The list of possible improvements and pending customization projects forms one of the components of what is called, by convention, the post-implementation review. Typically, this process should take place a few months (from three to six) after the project has been formally wrapped up; this means that the review should wait until after software processing has been completely transferred to company users and support personnel.

The contracted consultants normally put themselves at the disposal of the company to conduct this review, often at no additional charge. The hours may have already been charged during the project, or the possibility of future service opportunities may justify the consultant investing time to maintain contact with the client. Or perhaps the consulting firm will propose this service as a part of its quality control efforts. However this process is initiated, it is important that two types of people be involved in this review: those who have actively participated in the implementation project and those who understand the software intimately. This team will conduct an analysis of the benefits already achieved, of problems that will eventually require solutions, and possible improvements that can add greater value to the system.

The following activities should be considered in this review:

- interviewing several users who operate the system to check such factors such as ease of use, flexibility, performance, problems, and actual use of the available functionalities;
- interviewing informatics personnel to evaluate system performance, interruptions, vendor support (for the software package and components of the technological environment), and the degree of support demanded by users; and
- surveying software functionalities that are available but still are not used by company personnel.

This last activity merits a more detailed explanation. Comprehensive and integrated software offers a range of functionalities and an ample set of alternatives. During Phases 1 and 2, when we defined how the package would be implemented in the company, it is common to establish that certain more sophisticated functionalities, or those not directly applicable to the company's business, are to be frozen for future reevaluation. The decision to suspend functionality is normally associated with limitations imposed by the time frame of the project, or even by the acknowledgment that the company's personnel are not yet ready for the qualitative leap these functionalities represent. In the latter case the postimplementation review team would already have prior knowledge of these circumstances and seek to verify whether the time has come to propose activating some of the unused functions.

Other functionalities may not be used for different reasons. Users might not be aware of the functions, or they might abandon the functions because they do not perceive that the functions add value to their work. In either case, interviewing users will give the team an understanding of what is occurring and will serve as a basis for formulating recommendations.

The postimplementation review can be completed in a few days or in several weeks. What is most important is that a clear diagnosis of the actual utilization of the system be made, indicating

- benefits achieved,

- benefits partially achieved,

- problems and their causes,

- potential improvements,

- measures to be taken immediately,

- the expectation of additional results, and

- recommendations for how to proceed.

The revision process should—and must—be conducted again on future occasions, at greater time intervals (once a year) as a way of constantly evaluating the software, as well as not allowing the commitment to maintain the integrity of the package fade with the passage of time, or the whys and wherefores of certain business changes or processes be forgotten.

Simplifying

The problem of our time is that the future is not what it used to be.
—Paul Valéry

It is possible that since the idea arose to acquire a software package, some in the company have believed that implementing a new system would bring about simplification (read "lower costs, less bureaucracy, more agility") of internal business processes. This would, consequently, affect the structure of the business, which would also become simpler, having fewer hierarchical levels. During the project, the consultants have probably dealt with this question in workshops and meetings with the Executive Committee. The activities of prototyping the use of the package probably indicated the potential for simplifying things or eliminating unnecessary functions or tasks.

But since the project was still in development and all of these changes would depend on the effective implementation of the software and new procedures, this business objective (the simplification of the structure and processes) acquired a status of a desire or a perspective. After all, during the project, when new responsibilities are added to the everyday activities of the company and few changes can be carried out, the company needs manpower to handle the workload. Thus a reduction in man-hours, the elimination of tasks, and the reduction of intermediary positions become things for the future.

Now that the software is up and running, it is time to take up the idea again, this time for real. The potential reductions should be reassessed so that a careful and definitive analysis can be made to determine the measures to be taken to transform this potential into reality.

This assessment can take two forms:

- Perhaps a more profound study is conducted during the project (at times called Reengineering, with a capital R), and a detailed model is produced showing how the company should restructure and organize itself from here on out, with the only thing lacking being the task of implementing such a model.

- Or maybe a limited study is done, and the potential reductions indicated are based more on the experience of the project consultants than on a complete technical foundation. In truth, perhaps the project seeks to simplify the structure and the processes a little, but only insofar as the processes are directly associated with the implementation of the package (reengineering, with a small r).

In the first case, the project work plan is designed to cover specific restructuring tasks, eventually involving an additional phase—before the implementation project begins—which will be totally dedicated to this endeavor. The consulting team relies on people experienced in change processes on this level of magnitude.

In the second case it is also necessary to obtain the participation of consultants who specialize in organizational change, but the tasks of revising the company's processes and structure permeate the phases of the project as previously described.

In the first approach, the software package is the tool that, once available, permits implementation of the new predefined business model. The second approach starts from the principle that the package implementation will permit the structuring of a new model tied to the functionalities and business processes to be provided by the new system.

Generally, the first case leads to longer, more involved projects that seek more permanent results (if such are possible in today's world). In the second case, benefits are expected to be obtained by simply implementing the package with only limited changes, and then allowing for the possibility that, starting with this implementation, a cycle of continuous improvements will begin.

In the second case the company must think about starting a new project once the implementation is completed. This time the objective will be to define and implement organizational changes of greater impact in order to maximize the potential made possible by the new system.

Contacts with Other Companies That Use the Same Package

When the company decides to acquire a specific software package, it becomes a member of a club, the club of the package's users formed by companies (several, dozens, hundreds, or thousands) to which this solution also seemed to fit well. This reality cannot be ignored. On the contrary, it should be very well exploited.

Such a club can exist either formally or virtually. The formal club is called the user group, and it is sponsored and promoted by the software vendor. It meets regularly, having a Committee of Representatives (a few groups even have a headquarters, normally located in the facilities of one of the users). The club keeps its participant members informed about new developments and plans regarding the package and facilitates the exchange of experiences among user companies. Some user groups even help sell the package to potential clients, with the intention of increasing the package's installed base and, in so doing, maintaining the financial health of the vendor. The existence of a user group is a good sign; it leads one to expect that there will be greater ease in resolving certain problems with the software. This group can be more effective than individual companies in pressuring the vendor to invest in improving and updating the product.

A large user group ends up creating a small market of professionals who become experienced in the particular software package, or who specialize in the technology employed by the product. With the passage of time, as the installed base grows, these professionals end up being increasingly valued by the market.

The virtual club, on the other hand, is not structured, but information and experiences are exchanged nevertheless, even without the sponsorship of the vendor, and, at times, unbeknownst to the vendor.

Other user companies that have gone through the software package implementation process should be considered a resource that can yield excellent results if it is well exploited. Contacts with users and technicians of user companies can provide information that validates the assumptions of the company's project, bring understanding to what did not work and why, determine the extent of participation by in-house personnel, help configure the equipment, help gather opinions on the consultants (see Chapter 14), and identify some restrictions in functionality.

But a company should not approach this opportunity egoistically; instead it should act from the first moment with exchange in mind. It must never just soak up the maximum possible and then disappear. Each company that has already implemented the package has invested a great deal of money to get to where it is, and it intends to maximize the return on its investment. The company should seek to learn about the aspects of the product its club colleague intends to exploit and evaluate whether its project could help the other company's initiative. Who knows, maybe another company will allocate the time of one of its users who is experienced in the software to collaborate in your project.

A relationship created with some software user companies should be looked at not as something short term, but rather as a long-term commitment, in which all have much to gain by, for example, defining a new customization whose cost can be shared by several companies interested in the same solution; or perhaps there is a functionality that your company would be forced to pay for as a customization but, upon discovering that various others also have the same problem, as a group the companies may be able to convince the vendor to introduce such a functionality into a new product version (at no additional costs).

Also the company should be ready to receive and meet requests for visits from other companies interested in acquiring the software or obtaining information on how the project was conducted. To whatever extent possible, the company should serve all. Remember how many doubts and discussions your company faced internally until the package finally started operation. To be able to help other companies with your hard-earned experience is good for the ego as well. It is a way of verifying that your company has learned and is evolving professionally from the experience it went through in implementing the system.

13

My Dear Package Vendor: We're Counting on You

What to Expect from the Package Vendor
Now That the System Is Working

Expect the best, prepare for the worst, and take what comes.
—Chinese proverb

Let's recall the reasons that the company decided to acquire and implement the selected software package. Among other things, the company wanted to outsource the responsibility for developing and maintaining information systems that are essential to the business (but are not the company's business or specialty), so that the company could focus on the essence of its own operations.

This means that the company should expect this package, now called a system, to remain operating for several years, especially given that the company is paying an annual maintenance fee that exists principally to finance functional and technical improvements that will keep the product updated and in harmony with additional business requirements that will develop over time.

The field of technology is highly dynamic. New hardware and software is introduced all the time. Statistics show that every eighteen months (with increasing frequency) processing changes radically, expanding capacity and possible uses in business. This means two things: First, the company, not being a software producer cannot, by itself, follow this dynamic situation and prevent its systems from becoming obsolete. Second, the vendor must invest a great deal in the package to ensure that it continues maintaining the characteristics and facilities that made it the exceptional tool the company chose to support its business.

Therefore, the package vendor must have a sufficiently profitable operation to maintain its financial solidity and the capacity to permanently invest in research and development, if it is to remain competitive in the market. This is why some user groups help vendors sell their packages to new clients—because by so doing they are also taking care of their own futures as software users.

Good financial capacity is still not sufficient by itself. The vendor must also have on its payroll professionals involved in the development of the product who can orient these investments in the best possible manner, giving priority to improvements that produce the greatest added value to the package. And where are these professionals going to find inspiration for such decisions? In several places:

- in the installed base of the package, the clients, who have practical experience in running the product and who can point out package limitations and necessary additional functionalities;

- from direct competitors that introduce novelties in their products that must be quickly equaled by the vendor so that the package does not become obsolete;

- from management gurus and specialists in business administration who publish papers, introduce debates, and present seminars on their ideas;

- through perceiving the implications of new technologies that become available in the market and their possibilities when associated with the vendor's software packages;

- in legislative and economic changes that affect the package database and require management of new information for making business decisions; and

- through business tendencies (not fads) that modify the characteristics of company information systems and create important competitive differences.

If the package vendor knows how to work these aspects well, it not only will be successful in the software market; it will really deserve to receive the annual maintenance fee the user company has contracted to pay.

As a software package user, the company hopes the vendor will improve the product's functionality (providing greater agility for internal company processes), continue to align the product with legal and economic changes (obligatory information, economic indicators, and so forth), and keep the package technologically up-to-date (in terms of performance, operational ease, greater automation, connectivity, and so forth).

Will the Company's Package Vendor Survive in this Volatile Market?

The first commandment of management is that the driving force in new product development in not technology, not even money but, rather, people's imagination.

—David Packard

It is very difficult to say whether a company's package vendor will be able to stay the course. The dynamism of the technology market does not encourage blindly betting on anyone. Changes are radical and rapid, and the ability to maintain a profitable operation must be renewed every year (or every quarter in some cases). When we were still at the beginning of the process of selecting a software package, we tried to analyze certain marketing factors associated with each package vendor that presented itself as offering a prospective solution for the company. Evaluating the financial solidity and capability of the vendor was, without a doubt, one of our concerns.

To survive in this crazy technological market, money is just the start. Without it there is no way to invest in research and development, or to maintain an appropriate marketing and sales structure. Beyond that, rare and expensive individual talent drives this market. Behind the great software packages, just as for other great high-tech products introduced into the market, lie a few geniuses who represent a set of qualities not easily found in the average professional. These people are worth a great deal (read "high salaries and benefits"), they are aware of their worth, and, generally, they seek to associate their names only with enterprises that enjoy continual success. Maintaining such talent in firms that produce software packages is one of the chief tasks of the package vendor's CEO. It becomes a little easier if the CEO is one of these people, because he or she may be less likely to suffer with an excessively proud ego, the type that makes someone arrogant and blind to the problems of his or her own personnel and clients. If the package vendor is not so lucky, sooner or later the vendor's business will run into problems and eventually deteriorate.

Therefore, when analyzing a package vendor, one needs to determine whether the proper conditions are present for the vendor to survive with dignity in the technology market:

- profitability;

- investment capacity;

- the quality of key professionals in the firm;

- the participation of top management in the development of products,[1]

- the strategic importance given to the research and development sector of the company;

- the degree of present client satisfaction;

- a positive opinion about the company and products by the most influential market analysts;

- technological partnerships maintained with other technology companies that are leaders in their field of activities; and

- product focus.

---

1. I once heard a very interesting phrase on the importance of this point: Never trust a software vendor whose CEO cannot do the demo!

This last point—product focus—is very significant. A comprehensive and integrated software package, by itself, requires a respectable degree of investment and a great volume of work for the product to remain up-to-date and competitive. A vendor that looks on this package as only another of its many products will, necessarily, need to divide its capacity to invest and its management between the various items or services it is selling. For this strategy to be feasible, the size and profitability of the organization must truly permit the sharing of resources appropriately, as well as the dedication of sufficient time and intelligence to the package. This is especially true in cases where the package vendor also seeks to sell, in addition to the product, implementation services for the product. A consulting structure is another business, with different characteristics and another type of personnel; it also requires money to recruit and train staff, as well as to develop methodology and support tools. All these activities will detract attention and resources from the package itself.

In contrast, there is the vendor who totally depends on a single product. All of its attention, resources, and hopes are directed toward this product. If, on the one hand, this seems risky (never put all your eggs in one basket), on the other, it is a formula that can guarantee the future success of the package in the market (and in the user company).

In conclusion, there are no absolute guarantees in the technology market. There are only conditions that should be monitored to ensure that they remain favorable and give the software package vendor a reasonable shot at continuing to exist and evolve independently.

Technology not only allows us to do things more quickly and better; it permits us to radically change the way we do things, and through this change it creates new business and destroys the old (and, at times, the not so old). For example, while I am writing this book, some market analysts are already bringing up the hypothesis that, in the future, software packages will not exist in the form we know them today. They argue that a technology like the Internet (an indisputable phenomenon in the work of technology and communications) has permitted the creation in companies of an Intranet mentality—something such as limiting a portion of the Internet to private use, still in the process being born—that will make many functionalities of present packages obsolete. This is because it will force people to substitute the way information flow is now generated by market software with interactive processes that allow everyone to work together at the same time on a business process. As you can imagine, this resource will affect not only software packages but the very way that a company organizes its business.

The message is the following: One should not become complacent, thinking that the company's problems have been solved for some time to come. It is necessary to associate with business partners who also are aware of this reality and feel they need to constantly strive to maintain themselves above water.

14

Some Additional Ideas

Lessons Learned through Experience

You can only be one of two things in life: part of the problem, or part of the solution.
—Eldridge Cleaver

In this chapter I have gathered some ideas and suggestions from companies that have already gone through the experience of selecting and implementing a software package. These companies can provide lots of tips, many of which can be learned directly by visiting installations where packages your company is evaluating are being used (provided your company has established a good relationship with the other companies from the beginning—one that demonstrates interest in exchanging, and not just soaking up, ideas).

Creating an Environment for Software Vendors to Install Their Product

To create the right technological environment means checking very early on in the process to see how the vendor of the software package is organized to install its product and the degree of difficulty this installation represents. Moreover, end users should also be allowed to have contact with

173

the product and give their initial impressions. Some companies see this as a way to anticipate problems and evaluate the vendor's support personnel more thoroughly.

But it is not always feasible to put this idea into practice, because the requirements for installing the product in the company's facilities can demand time and entail prohibitive costs. First of all, adequately configured equipment must be available at the company's facility, and this generally is not the case. Thus an equipment vendor also willing to participate in the evaluation may have to be involved.

Also, in order for the package to be used by in-house personnel for exploratory purposes, a minimum database would need to be constructed so that users can navigate through the system.

In practice, what we are seeing are software vendors and consulting firms that invest in prototyping or benchmarking environments (for performance evaluation) in their own organizations. They set up these testing sites in order to demonstrate to potential clients that a particular package can be an excellent solution. The typical environment consists of machines, the software itself, partially configured, and support personnel to help the client better understand and test the package (the vendor might even charge for this service).

The existence of such a prototyping environment is a good sign, because it demonstrates the vendor's commitment to, and investment in, the product. Furthermore, if this environment can be made available for other types of activities, such as training company professionals to be assigned to the project, the time line for implementing the software could be accelerated.

Interviewing Consultants When the Implementation Proposal Is Being Developed

Independent of the credentials that a consulting firm presents, which attest to its ability to successfully implement the chosen software package, many companies maintain that the most important piece of information is who, specifically, will be assigned to the particular project, because this will make the difference. It is fundamental to have consultants assigned who have experience in the type of project (package implementations) and in the product (the specific package).

By informing the consulting firm of the company's desire to interview and get to know the consultants who are to be assigned to the project, in the event of approval, the company can start to evaluate two important points. First, it can determine whether the consulting firm has already thought about who it will assign to the project, if it has personnel available for the job (which is not always the case), and if the professionals involved in selling the firm's consulting services also will be participating in the project (that is, if they can deliver what they are trying to sell). Next, it is wise to determine if the professionals to be assigned from the consulting firm really possess the qualifications and seniority appropriate for the project and the contracting company. Personnel turnover in consulting firms is high, and those whose credentials impress prospective clients do not always stick around long enough for their experience to be taken advantage of by new clients.

But one need not be radical in this analysis, for ideal conditions do not exist. The consulting firm can actually be highly qualified for the service and not have, at the moment, an adequate team on hand—owing to the very success of its present projects. If the consulting firm's sales representatives know how to relate the true facts appropriately, they can transform a temporary limitation into a strong sales tool, unequaled by their competitors.

Requesting Names of Qualified Consultants from Other Companies

Here is another interesting recommendation: When visiting a client who is already using a software package that is under examination as a possible option for the company, if such a client speaks highly of the consulting firm that developed the implementation project, why not ask exactly who were the marvelous consultants responsible? Get the names of those on the team who brought about this success. With these names in hand, the company can approach the consulting firm and ask if its project can count on these same highly valued professionals. Even if it is not possible to commit these people to the company's project, those trying to sell the consulting firm's services will feel compelled to present professionals with equivalent resumes. All this is a way of demonstrating the degree of quality the company demands, and it must be taken into serious consideration by the firm that wishes to be awarded the service contract to implement the package.

Another source that can be used to obtain names of qualified consultants is the package software vendor. The vendor normally tracks the implementation work done around its product and usually provides training for consulting firm personnel. So the vendor gets to know who is who in consulting. But be aware that the vendor generally tries not to involve third parties in its sales process. (After all, its primary objective is to sell the package—and from then on the problem becomes one of a different order.) Thus a vendor will get involved in recommending a consulting firm only if it detects a means of winning a favorable decision for its proposal. Therefore it can be to the company's advantage to consider the vendor when evaluating consulting firms.

Workshops and Meetings Outside the Company

When accompanied by good conversations, the work flows happily.
—Schiller

As we have mentioned several times previously, the package implementation project will add to the daily workload of everyone in the company. All operations will continue as before, but now the company will face an additional challenge—putting the software into operation—so that the business work environment can be simplified and become more effective and efficient. For this to occur, the company must call upon the users to participate in various meetings and workshops. Frequently this will take up their entire workday and, during some project phases, a lot more than that.

Experience demonstrates that using the company's in-house facilities to conduct such meetings and workshops is not always the best course. Most employees start the day by going by their desks before the meeting, or they do this at lunch time, and then they can become involved in problems and working on pending tasks. The result: They end up neglecting the principal objective of the day, in the name of putting out fires. Inadequate dedication at such a crucial juncture can generate major aftereffects, such as not having the right people involved in making certain key decisions during the initial project phases.

The recommendation, then, is to remove people from their work environment, send them to a location outside the company, a place where the only possible option is to concentrate on the situation at hand. Although this represents an additional project expense (rent for a meeting site, lunches and transportation expenses), those who defend this option maintain that such costs are amply compensated by the more efficient use of the time, and the contribution this makes to keeping the project timetable on track.

I would maintain that an additional advantage exists: Gathering the personnel outside the company helps to increase group spirit (team building) so necessary to the project's development. It allows for greater contact between consultants and in-house personnel, and it creates an informal climate allowing for healthy interchange in order to counterbalance the responsibilities and challenges that lie ahead for all those involved.

Making these days outside the company truly different—for example, asking for informal attire, a combination of work and recreation, a banquet to close these activities—contributes greatly to establishing a favorable environment for the project and creates greater expectations regarding the results to be obtained (for this reason leaders should avoid exaggerations so that expectations remain realistic).

Evaluating the Software Package Documentation

The package's documentation is an important tool for the postimplementation period. It should be used to remove minor doubts that arise during day-to-day operation, before resorting to support services, and such documentation will also help in training future users hired by the company, be this to increase the work force or to substitute for workers who leave.

Today packages depend less and less on documentation, in the traditional sense of the expression—namely, those thick, detailed manuals that describe how the system works. The destiny of such manuals has always been to sit on bookshelves and lend little support in system processing, or they are sent off to the technical library in the informatics sector, where no user ever consults them.

More practical, nowadays, is what we call *online documentation*. This consists of descriptions and explications that are part of the system and organized such that, from any point within the package, one can access information associated with a particular operation being performed. This mode of help makes the support process more attractive to the user (who does not have to go search the manuals to locate information on the subject, which is not always an easy task). It also makes this process more effective, because the user continues interacting with the system to clear up doubts, thus adding to the credibility of the package.

Companies that have gone through documentation evaluation recommend checking on three points that can make a difference:

- Is the documentation easy to read?

- Does the documentation provide practical examples of system use, so that reading and learning is facilitated?

- Is the documentation automatically updated when a new version of the software package is released?

Requesting a Trial Period with the Product

Engaging in a trial period is an interesting idea. Let's presume that the selection process has gone well and that there is a consensus regarding the choice of a software package. But in order to be sure that the corresponding commitment of resources and effort will yield the expected return, the company decides to try out the product for a certain time, and only thereafter will it confirm its choice.

This trial probably will not be free. But some companies that can allow for this additional analysis time realize that such an investment is worthwhile, and they consider this idea an excellent solution for making a sound decision.

In practice, undergoing a trial period involves conducting a small implementation project, upon which rigid limitations are imposed so that the work can be carried out in a short time frame (generally, over one to three months). During such a trial period, some parties who might be called upon to conduct the full-blown project installation later on are involved, such as consultants, key users, and specialists, affording a chance for everyone to observe them in action.

This approach is similar to that presented earlier in the chapter, where we explored creating an environment for the package vendor to install its product. With a trial period, the process becomes more formal and definitive. It might be that the equipment question, for example, has been resolved or is on the way to being resolved.

What has been referred to as rigid limitations in the context of the trial run implementation project could mean one or more of the following things:

- testing only a part of the functionality (one module, for example);
- concentrating the work on only one part of the business (a product line, factory, a type of operation, or a specific group of people);
- simplifying a series of facts, abolish exceptions, in order to work as if the conditions were ideal;
- not being concerned about interfaces with other systems; and,
- not using real data, just conducting simulations.

The package vendor and the consultants do not always agree on employing this type of evaluation, and sometimes they try to dissuade the company from the idea. The reason: work of this nature presents lots of risks that can be underestimated by the company, because of a lack of experience. The greatest among these is the viability of establishing the required limitations so that the trial period can occur within the projected time and with the expected results. For several more sophisticated packages, the preparation of a minimal processing environment requires a volume of work and data definitions on an order equivalent to that required to develop the entire full-blown project implementation itself.

In this event, it is more reasonable to try to get through the question of product evaluation by reverting to other guarantees that make the company feel secure enough to contract the implementation process. One thing is certain: There is no way to contract for a software package and an implementation project without sharing some degree of risk with the other parties to the contract. Total exemption from risk simply does not exist. For this reason, we have tried to demonstrate the importance of involving all key people from the start of the process, for this is a business challenge that can only be resolved with the broad collaboration of all involved.

Setting Up an Internal Support Structure for the Software

Establishing a means of supporting users with an internal support structure is vital. When we recommended that the company prepare itself to operate the software on its own, once the implementation project has been concluded, emphasis was placed on the users and technicians involved in the project learning about the product and the aims of the implementation so that they could assume responsibility for the processing of the new system. This responsibility covers not only the placement and extraction of business data into the system, but also the infrastructure that ensures software processing continuity.

Some companies believe that since they already have an internal support structure for existing systems, the arrival of a new system simply requires increasing the scope of such work, as an extension of existing service patterns. In other words, the company has experience in maintaining systems in operation and it believes the recently implemented software will not add any significant additional difficulties.

Yet when a company is dealing with a comprehensive and integrated software package, along with a new technological infrastructure, the solution may not be so simple. There are many new aspects to take into account, as well as an environment that is completely different, that must be supported from here on out. Although the company may have an excellent track record for serving users, its structure may not be organized adequately for the new reality.

The suggestion is to start the work of organizing this support structure while the project is still in progress, choosing certain in-house professionals who have stood out in the group because of their enthusiasm, dedication, and knowledge of the new system. These will be the people who can lend a hand in developing a support structure. The company will need to define whether this new support structure is to be inserted into the existing user support organization, or whether it is to form a new and separate functional sector. It will need to plan how many people should be assigned to support tasks, their positions and responsibilities, the type of know-how such a structure requires, whether support should be available twenty-four hours a day or in a more limited form. The company will also need to qualify the types of support that will be needed in the new functional, technological, and telecommunications environment. Whether new people should be hired from outside is another question. (At this moment, executives of consulting firms have an uneasy feeling because their personnel are naturally targeted for recruitment by their clients.)

Some companies transform the need to create a software package support structure into an internal marketing opportunity. From the beginning of the project they make a hot line available to provide information about the project and the new system. This can be the telephone extension of a key project person, or an E-mail address where questions and concerns can be raised by anyone interested in the project or package. Gradually, this hot line will assume help line proportions, as the project advances and concerns, or problems, become more specific and require more elaborate responses, or even study of a better alternative solution.

Developing an internal support structure for the software package is also a way of limiting the company's dependence on its technology suppliers to that which is really of interest and that which generates true benefits and savings. If the company does not concern itself with providing the support naturally required by a sophisticated software package, then it will have to incur expenses by paying third parties (consultants, specialists, and the package vendor) to carry out a series of activities that could have been conducted using in-house resources, at a lesser expense. It is important to note that, with rare exceptions, providing such basic support activities does not attract much interest on the part of the other parties to the project implementation contract. Support activities lie outside their commercial focus, and the prospect of permanently providing such services does not motivate their professional employees. This combination of negative points can only be compensated in a single manner: paying the higher fees charged to provide such services.

Do Not Underestimate the Importance of Managing the Project

The topic of project management has been brought up at various points through the book. It is not enough just to have the world's best software and an effective group of clever people to implement it; it is vital to plan, organize, and carry out the work to achieve the company's objective.

The recommendations of companies, in this regard, is to be aware of something that is not always so clear, even at the highest levels of the organization. A complex project, like the implementation of a software package, must be managed by using proven administrative techniques, control tools, and leadership capacity. It must also be based on appropriate practical experience, discipline, and the ability to be flexible.

Therefore, when evaluating who its partners are to be, and who among the employee ranks is to be assigned to develop the software package implementation project, company decision makers should consider the factor of capacity to administer the projects as a question that merits a certain weight when comparing the various candidates to lead the project. Checking how the candidates are positioned with respect to many of the factors that have been discussed and described in this book is one way of conducting such an evaluation and of confirming whether the qualifications presented in the proposals, or the names suggested to carry them out, truly merit complete confidence.

Conclusion

A successful business software package implementation requires, above all, partnership. Corporate managers, information technology staff, key users and end users of information technology, external business consultants, trainers, and specialists—all must team up in order to create the best possible conditions to achieve project success. The project is successful if it provides tangible and significant benefits for the company, brings a good return on investment, and warrants professional satisfaction among the ones who have dedicated their time and knowledge to make it happen.

But on what does this success depend the most? Maybe now you have your own conclusion. But consider this: the project success depends on details. Yes, the little things that are not discussed in the boardroom, maybe not clearly described in the work plan, and certainly thought of as only "part of the job." I'm talking about day-to-day issues that are apparently very small or not significant on their own. Details that seem to be just part of the responsibility of someone on the project team, or inherent to a difficult task, and sooner or later will be solved. Those are the details that, if not properly managed, can lead to delays, design failures, insufficient testing, poor system performance, lack of documentation, and other undesirable situations.

Some of the details we have in mind can be illustrated through questions such as the following:

- What is this column, in this table, used for?

- What software functions are affected by the different parameters of this field?

- What makes the system respond with a better or worse performance?

- What is the best way to document the workshops conducted with the users?

- How can we can make sure that all professionals involved in the project feel that they are being treated as important participants?

- What is the best way to document processes that have been redesigned, in order to get them approved *and* help the users understand them?

- When can the project team decide, and when is it imperative to send the problem to a higher authority?

- Who is the best person working at the software vendor to solve this specific technical issue?

- How should transaction security and process automation be balanced in order to minimize manual procedures? And there are hundreds of other possible questions.

The only way of dealing properly with all the details is by allocating the right people to the implementation project—people with product knowledge, similar project experience, command of the methodology, planning and managing capabilities, technological environment support experience, the initiative to make decisions, good communication skills, the ability to handle details, awareness of the importance of documentation, and leadership skills all must exist within an implementation team.

The human factor is the engine driving a successful software project. Even the best business software package running over state-of-the-art technology is totally dependent on how people are able to implement it and use it to create significant benefits for a company. Having the best people is even more important than selecting the best package. Outstanding people can maximize the results of an integration project even when the software is not outstanding. The opposite is not true.

So when planning a software implementation project, make sure that the company has a trusted team. If necessary, postpone the start date until everyone is confident that the company has the best possible group of professionals. Good luck on your project!

Index